My Life in Crazytown

How I Turned ADHD Into My Superpower

Richard Lowe

The Writing King

My Life in Crazytown: How I Turned ADHD Into My Superpower

DISCLAIMER

This book is about my childhood, and my childhood was not appropriate for children. If you've read this far you already know that, but I'll say it plainly: physical abuse, sexual abuse, emotional violence, and parents who were at best incompetent and at worst predatory. I've written it the way it happened, not the way you might prefer it happened.

I'm not interested in a forgiveness arc. I'm not angry, I didn't forgive, and I don't spend my days in therapy working through it. I spent my days building something out of it. That's the story.

Read it or don't.

Table of Contents

See books by Richard Lowe at

https://masterofworlds.com

Get free publishing insights and industry updates at

https://thewritingking.substack.com

For ghostwriting and book coaching services see

https://thewritingking.com

Prologue: Welcome to Crazytown

This is not a story about overcoming adversity. It's not about finding inner peace or learning to forgive. It's about something far more practical: how to turn the worst things that happen to you into the best things about you.

I spent the first nineteen years of my life in what I now call Crazytown, a place where nothing made sense, where the rules changed without warning, and where the people who were supposed to protect you were often the ones you needed protection from. It was a landscape of emotional warfare, silent treatments, and violence both threatened and delivered.

Most people who grow up in Crazytown become permanent residents. They learn to navigate the chaos, to manage the damage, to cope with the ongoing effects of trauma. Some become casualties. Others become survivors. A few get therapy and learn to heal.

I took a different path. I became an architect.

Not the kind who designs buildings, but the kind who designs solutions. I learned to take the wreckage of a dysfunctional childhood and build something useful from the debris. The hypervigilance that trauma creates became my edge in reading complex systems. The systematic thinking I developed to predict and avoid my father's explosions became my ability to design elegant software solutions. The emotional distance that complicated relationships became my objectivity as an editor and ghostwriter.

What looked like damage was raw material.

This is the story of how a scared, awkward kid who couldn't make friends and didn't fit anywhere discovered that being different wasn't a bug. It was a feature. How the same traits that made me a "difficult child" made me an exceptional problem-solver. How the intensity my family tried to suppress became the engine that drove decades of professional success.

I didn't overcome my challenges. I weaponized them.

The kid who collected everything became an adult who could see patterns others missed. The teenager who exploded when touched became a man who set firm boundaries and demanded respect. The college dropout who couldn't sit still in class became the executive who could focus for hours on complex problems.

This is not a redemption story because I was never broken to begin with. This is a recognition story: the moment when you realize that what everyone told you was wrong with you is what's most right about you.

If you've ever felt like you don't fit, if you've ever been told you're too much or too little, if you've ever wondered whether the things that make you different might make you valuable, this book is for you.

Welcome to Crazytown. The exit is closer than you think.

Introduction

In the *Star Trek: The Next Generation* episode "Loud as a Whisper," the Enterprise meets Riva, a deaf mediator who has spent his career resolving conflicts across the galaxy. Riva doesn't see his deafness as a disability; he has turned it into his greatest professional asset. He uses telepathic interpreters to communicate, and his condition forces others to slow down, be deliberate, think before they speak. His silence creates space for understanding.

When Riva's interpreters are killed in an attack, he is shattered. How can a deaf man without his interpreters mediate between warring factions if he cannot be heard? Then he realizes the truth: his deafness is not the obstacle; it is the solution. He teaches both sides sign language, forcing them to learn a shared mode of communication. In struggling together to understand him, they begin to understand each other.

I watched this as an adult and saw myself in Riva. Like him, I spent years believing my differences were obstacles. Like him, I was wrong.

This is the story of living in Crazytown and realizing that the analytic habits I learned to survive the chaos are the same tools other people need to make sense of their own.

Chapter 1: First Blood

My transformation started before I could even speak, before I could breathe.

My mother said she went into labor on a plane back from the Philippines and delivered at Travis Air Force Base. It sounded dramatic, but there was probably truth in it.

My father was an Air Force radio operator stationed overseas. He met Mom while on leave in Vacaville, California. They spent time in the Philippines, where my mother gave birth to my sister, Debbie.

Debbie died at nine months, and something fundamental in my mother broke. A year and a half later we returned to the States, my mother carrying me and all that unresolved anguish.

By six, my father had left the Air Force for a civil service job as a graphics artist, technical illustrations and charts: precision and control, which seemed to define him.

I wonder if I was meant to replace what they'd lost, to fill the hole that Debbie's death had torn in my mother's life. If so, I failed before I even took my first breath.

My father? I still question whether he had any part in Debbie's death. I'll never know. Time and an ocean bury the answer, but the doubt persists. Given what he did later, and what my mother said he tried while she was pregnant with me, the question feels less paranoid than it sounds.

He grabbed her and slammed her abdomen against a dresser, aiming for me. It's a miracle I survived. I was one tough little baby, as later events would prove. I was fighting for my life before I was born; my mother's body the only barrier between me and his violence.

I was born blue. My blood was trying to kill me. The delivery room must have been chaos: alarms, shouted orders, my mother watching as her second baby arrived already dead. Within minutes, they drained my blood and replaced it. My mother's negative Rh factor had turned her womb into a war zone; I was the casualty. It was a miracle of modern medicine that they brought me back from death.

That total blood replacement reads like a rehearsal for what came next. I would spend my childhood having my emotional system drained and rebuilt from scratch, one trauma at a time.

Those first months, my baby book tells a different story. My mother's handwriting bounces with happiness, loops and curves of joy. "Richard smiled today." "He is such a delightful baby." "Jerry loves holding him." She documented every milestone like a scientist recording a miracle. The woman writing those entries had no idea what was coming.

The Early Experiments

The lithium tasted like a penny. I was two, bouncing off furniture, climbing bookshelves, turning every surface into a launchpad. The doctor's office smelled like disinfectants and fear. My parents sat in plastic chairs, watching me ricochet like a human pinball.

"It's not working," Mom said, her voice tight with exhaustion. The bags under her eyes had become permanent fixtures.

"Give it more time," the doctor replied, but his tone suggested he already knew better.

Eight months later, they switched tactics. Sugar became my new medication.

By seven, the routine was automatic: four sodas before lunch, chocolate bars melting in my pockets, rolls of Life Savers making my teeth ache. The good candy and gum came in plastic containers shaped like telephones and treasure chests. My fingers worked the tiny latches while my tongue anticipated the rush.

"Richard, slow down," Mom would say, watching me tear through the grocery store aisles.

But slowing down felt impossible. The world moved too slowly, adults talked too much, and standing still made my skin crawl. It felt like ants were marching under it.

My father's voice cut through everything. "Don't embarrass us. Children must always be quiet." The flat tone meant consequences if I did not comply.

I learned to swallow words before they could escape. I also learned to respect the belt.

The First Real Crack

The first real crack in the foundation came when I was nine months old.

It was evening, that restless time when babies get fussy and parents get frayed. I was screaming in my crib, hungry, tired, overwhelmed by whatever makes babies cry. My father stormed into the nursery with unusual fury.

"Shut up," he said, looming over the crib like a drill sergeant. His voice had that edge it got when patience evaporated.

I kept crying. What else does a nine-month-old do?

Dad's anger exploded. He grabbed a pillow from the rocker and pressed it over my face.

Even from that early age, I remember fragments: the weight blocking the light, the panic of no air, then a gasp. And what came after, the scene that replays in my head to this day.

"Jerry." My mother's voice from the doorway, sharp and quiet like a teacher catching a student cheating. Moments later I was in her arms; my father stood frozen, the pillow still in his hands.

"He wouldn't stop crying," my father said, his voice completely different now. Smaller. Defensive. The guilty look on his face was unmistakable: the expression of someone caught doing something unforgivable.

My mother looked at him for a long moment, her face unreadable. She could have screamed or demanded answers. Or she could have called someone, anyone, who might have helped. She could have left with me right then and never looked back.

Instead, she adjusted me on her hip, bouncing me gently, and said, "Maybe he's hungry."

That was it. No confrontation. No consequences. No acknowledgment of danger. Just a quiet agreement to pretend it hadn't happened. She was good at pretending. Protecting was something else.

The incident faded from memory. From nine months until I was six, life felt surprisingly normal on the surface. I played in the backyard with the neighbor kids, building elaborate dirt cities and staging battles with toy soldiers. I made friends easily, laughed often, and did all the regular kid stuff that fills up childhood memory books. My brain had apparently locked the murderous father away in a separate compartment, filing him under "anomaly" rather than "pattern."

That compartmentalization worked fine until the day it didn't.

The Rialto Education

The Rialto apartment smelled of swamp cooler dampness and cooking grease. The sidewalk was still wet, gray and smooth as glass. My bare feet slapped as I ran toward it, cement squelching between my toes. Handprints and footprints…my mark on something permanent.

The broken glass pile caught the California sun like scattered diamonds, amber beer bottles, clear window glass, and green Coca-Cola shards. I ran across it barefoot; sharp edges pressed into my soles without breaking skin. The sound was incredible: crunch, each step a percussion note that vibrated up through my legs.

"What are you doing?" Dad's voice, sharp with alarm.

"It feels good," I said, which was the truth and obviously the wrong answer.

The sensation was exactly what my brain craved: intense, immediate, impossible to ignore. Better than candy, better than anything.

But glass could be dangerous in ways I didn't understand yet. A scream cut through the afternoon like a siren. Blood soaked the grass, spreading in ways that made little sense. Her foot had found a broken bottle hidden in the green.

"Mom! MOM!" We were running before I knew it, her hand gripping mine, a blood trail behind us.

Mom appeared in the doorway, saw the blood, and her face went white.

"What happened? Oh God, what happened?"

"Broken bottle," I panted. "She stepped on a broken bottle."

I watched her sit on the edge of the tub, hands shaking as she wrapped gauze around her bleeding feet, white turning red in seconds.

I grabbed the towels. Mom grabbed the keys. We carried her to the car, leaving a trail of bloody footprints. The ER smelled like iodine. A nurse pressed down hard while the doctor stitched, thread tugging skin, my mother biting her lip and nodding that she was fine.

Even at five, I knew getting help meant explaining fast. Panic was a luxury.

We moved when the money got better, or worse. I could never tell. This new place had a swamp cooler on stilts, always dripping into soft earth. Bugs loved it: beetles, spiders, things that skittered when you moved the mud.

That's where I found the footlocker.

My heart hammered as I worked the latches. Pirate treasure; it had to be filled with gold coins, jeweled daggers, maybe a map with an X. My hands shook as the lid creaked open.

Inside were heavy metal objects. Round with pins. Long and pointed, balanced in my grip. Not coins, but weapons. The round ones had a serious weight as I tossed them palm to palm.

"Jesus Christ!" Dad's voice cracked like a whip. He ran toward me, terror twisting his face. "Drop those! Drop them RIGHT NOW!"

The objects hit the mud with dull thuds.

"What are they?" I asked, but Dad was already dragging me away from the cooler, his grip tight enough to bruise.

Later, when his breathing slowed: "Grenades. Live grenades and shells. Could've blown us all to pieces." I had made the most amazing discovery of my life, and somehow it was wrong.

Dad placed the grenades and 20mm bullets on an elevated shelf in the corridor. From time to time, I'd clamber up to inspect them. I don't think my dad had any idea I could climb like a monkey.

Later, before we moved to Stoddard Street, I watched Dad curiously from the window, wondering why he wanted me to stay in the house. He seemed so serious, and I wondered what he was doing.

He went to the pond, whose surface shimmered like a dull mirror, skimmed with green. Four white geese swam peacefully, heads dipping, tails tipping, small ripples widening to the reeds.

Dad crossed the yard with a steady, purpose-walk. No bucket. No feed. Just hands.

He stepped to the edge and reached. His fingers closed around the first neck. The goose thrashed, wings slapping water, a wet drumbeat against his sleeves. He twisted. Something in it gave with a soft, wrong sound, not loud enough for the movie version, just a click and a sigh. The body kept moving for a breath, wings fluttering, feet bicycling air, then the weight settled, heavy and loose.

He let it drop and reached for the next.

The second fought harder. There was hissing and the flat slap of wings. He twisted, and the head went at an angle that didn't belong on a living thing. The third tried to run, feet skittering on mud, a white streak against algae. He caught it anyway. Twist. Flutter. Stillness. The fourth stood with its head high as if it could think its way out. He took that one too.

The sounds stuck with me more than the sight, a hiss turning to a choking gurgle. Water slapping. The wingbeats that started frantic and fell to a soft patter, like a book closing repeatedly until it didn't. A final flutter. Then, the silence that felt too big for the yard.

My hands left prints on the window. My throat felt tight and small.

"Why did he do that?" I asked Mom.

She turned from the sink and followed my eyes. Her face went flat in the way adults' faces do when they are deciding what not to say. "I don't know, honey. I just don't know."

I kept watching the pond. White feathers drifted like torn paper. He was already walking back, calm, as if he had finished taking out the trash. I learned adults did things for reasons that made sense to them and no one else.

Real Men Don't Cry

I'd done something wrong. I forget what it was, but it upset my father, who was busy working on a commission from an officer at Norton Air Force Base.

The tears started the moment I saw his face change. Just a flicker across his features, but I knew what was coming.

I turned to Mom, hoping she'd intervene, but she just looked away, returning to her needlepoint. No help from her.

"I'm sorry, Dad. I'm really sorry." The words tumbled out in a rush, high-pitched and desperate. "I didn't mean to…"

"Real men don't cry." His voice was flat, final. He stood up from his chair with deliberate slowness, each movement a countdown.

I wiped my eyes with my sleeve, trying to force the tears back, but they kept coming anyway. The harder I tried to stop them, the faster they flowed. My chest hitched with the effort of holding back sobs.

"Please, I'll stop. I'm stopping, see?" But my voice cracked on the words, betraying me.

Dad's hand moved to his belt buckle. The metal clinked as he worked it loose, the leather sliding through the loops with a whisper that seemed to echo in the quiet room. He folded the belt in half, testing the weight in his palm.

"I warned you," he said, and I could hear disappointment mixing with something else in his voice. "Turn around."

My shoulders shook as I complied, the tears now streaming freely down my face. I pressed my lips together, trying to lock the crying inside, knowing that every sob would only make it worse.

I learned my father didn't approve of any emotional displays from any male children. Later in life, when my wife passed away, I couldn't even force myself to cry at her funeral. The conditioning was too severe.

I eventually learned another lesson. Mom wouldn't stand up to Dad. I never even knew if she agreed with him or just didn't want to become a target of his wrath herself.

Learning to Ride a Bike

The bike was too big for me, a hand-me-down from a neighbor kid whose parents had given up teaching him. The seat wobbled when I climbed on, and my feet barely reached the pedals.

"Just keep pedaling," Dad said, giving me a push that sent me careening down the sidewalk. "Don't think about it."

But thinking was all I could do as I aimed straight for the same oak tree that I'd hit nineteen times before. The impact rattled my teeth and sent me sprawling onto the concrete, skinning my knees and palms.

"Get back on," Dad called from twenty feet away. "You're not hurt."

I was hurt. My elbow bled, and my head rang from bouncing off the trunk. Crying would only make it worse.

I climbed back on and pedaled toward the same tree. Crash number twenty-one. Then twenty-two.

"What's wrong with you?" Dad's voice carried frustration and embarrassment. "Every other kid figures this out in an hour."

On attempt twenty-three, something clicked. My brain finally understood the physics of momentum and balance, the way forward motion created stability instead of destroying it. I sailed past the tree and down the entire block before figuring out how to stop.

"See?" Dad said when I wheeled back, grinning despite my collection of scrapes and bruises. "I told you it wasn't that hard."

Paint store incident

The paint store hit me like a wall of chaos as the automatic doors slid open. Color samples covered every surface, a rainbow that hurt to look at. Turpentine and chemical possibilities curled in the air. Fluorescent lights buzzed like angry wasps.

"Stay close," Dad said, already moving toward the counter with the focused intensity he brought to everything.

The overload scrambled my circuits: too many people moving at once, voices ricocheting off hard walls, paint cans clattering as employees restocked. My navigation short-circuited and I drifted into a maze of industrial shelving.

I spotted brown work pants by the paint mixer and grabbed the fabric like a life preserver, fingers locking while my brain tried to catch up.

"Excuse me, son, but you're not my kid."

I looked up. Kind eyes. A confused face. Not my father.

I screamed.

The sound knifed through the store like an alarm. Mom scooped me up. Dad hissed that I had embarrassed him. He then turned back to look at paint swatches, discussing each color in detail with mom.

What? I thought. No belt? I breathed a sigh of relief.

I learned something that day: crowded, complex places confused me, and confusion brought consequences.

Chores

Saturday, late afternoon. The kitchen smelled of Pine-Sol and spaghetti sauce. Sun slid across the linoleum in long gold strips. I was building a fort out of couch cushions when Mom called from the sink.

"Richard, in here."

I padded in, socks picking up crumbs. Plates were stacked like small towers by the faucet. The water ran hot, steam rising.

"It's time you start doing chores," she said, handing me a damp dish towel. Her tone was light, as if she were offering me something.

"Chores?" The word tasted like soap.

Dad came in from the garage, wiping his hands on a rag that smelled like oil. "Work ethic," he said, like a verdict. "You need to learn it."

Mom nodded toward the dishes. "You'll help. After dinner, you clear the table, scrape the plates, rinse, I'll wash, you dry." She pulled up a high chair for me to stand on.

I blinked at the stacks. "All of them?"

Dad's eyes held mine. Flat, certain. "All of them." I got the impression he was daring me to object.

Confusion prickled up my neck. I had plans. The fort. The Lego spaceship waiting on my bedroom floor. "Why?"

He set the rag on the counter, squared the salt and pepper without looking at them. "Allowance is not free. One dollar and twenty-five cents a week. You earn it."

My stomach dipped. "I have to work for money?"

"You work to make money," he said. "Life is hard. No handouts."

The faucet hissed. Mom pressed a plate into my hands. It was slick and hot. I almost dropped it. "Dry," she said, gentle. "Circle motions. Get the rim."

The towel scratched my fingers. The plate squeaked when I got it right. I stacked it in the cabinet with two hands; the weight was solid. Another plate. Another squeak. Forks clinked in the drawer like small bells.

Dad stood in the doorway, not hovering, not leaving. Watching. "Trash goes out on Tuesdays and Fridays," he said. "You haul it before school. Table cleared after every meal. No exceptions."

"What if I forget?" I asked and heard the smallness in my voice.

He didn't blink. "You do not forget. You put a note by your bed. You set an alarm. You do the work."

Something shifted as the stack of clean plates grew. The rhythm settled in. Scrape, rinse, dry, squeak, stack. My breath matched the motions. The kitchen calmed. I felt the line between messy and done. The towel warmed my hands.

By the time I tied off the trash bag, the plastic rasped my knuckles and smelled like orange peels and coffee grounds. The back door stuck a little, the night air cool on my face. I heaved the bag into the can and felt the small satisfaction of hearing it land.

Dad met me at the door. He held out a quarter, then another, then another, then a dime and a nickel. Cold coins. Real weight. He closed my fingers over them.

"You earned it," he said.

The confusion thinned. The rule clicked into place. I tucked the coins in a jar on my dresser and looked at them like they were proof. Work makes money. Do the work, get the money. Simple. Clean. No arguing with it.

I quickly found that I enjoyed the chores. They settled my mind and calmed my jittery nerves. Before long, I felt weird on the few occasions when I could skip chores. It was as if a pattern had become locked in my mind.

I clung to that rule like a life preserver. It steadied me when other rules made no sense. Years later, it would decide how I saved, how I built a career. I learned that night, in a kitchen that smelled like soap and tomatoes, that effort could be stacked and counted, and that certainty mattered.

It was also a ceiling. If money had to come from sweat, I could not see money that came from leverage. I turned down easy wins that felt unearned, distrusted passive income, and worked overtime instead of learning ownership. The rule kept me safe. It also kept me small.

Kindergarten

Mother loved books. Heavy maple bookshelves lined every wall in the living room, and each shelf was stuffed with encyclopedias, dictionaries, books, and countless women's magazines.

She passed her love of books on to me and my sister. They were the first thing she gave me that felt like a doorway. Dr. Seuss, then science, then history. She read until her voice went soft. By the time school loomed, I read everything I could hold open. Most of what I knew came from that living room and her hands.

Then she told me I was going to start school soon, something called kindergarten. School meant a room full of kids, rules I did not know, and a teacher who might be anything. As the day approached, my stomach tightened, my head throbbed, and my chest felt like a fist. I decided I did not want to go.

The morning arrived anyway. Mom pulled me from bed and set a bowl in front of me. The cereal went soggy while I stared at the clock. The last minutes slid away like soap in water.

At the door, I tried to be brave. Dad was at work, so I could afford the luxury of emotions. Tears came hot and fast. The fear tipped into noise. I kicked. I twisted. I tried to bolt to my room. Mom caught me and lifted. We moved down the sidewalk; me flailing in her arms, shoes scuffing her shins, my face wet.

We must have been quite a sight. The school doors opened, and the principal stood there, a kindly-looking older man with a gray crew cut and a calm face. He took the scene at a glance.

"Set him down," he said to my mother, voice even. "I'll take it from here."

I stopped crying. Something had changed.

Mom set me on the ground and left.

I gulped air and hiccupped. He reached for me, turned me neatly, and sat with me across his knee like it was the most normal thing in the world. A paddle appeared from a drawer.

The first swat landed with a flat, shocking sound. Heat bloomed across my backside. Another swat. He spoke as he did it.

This differed from the punishments from my father. The principal didn't act out of anger; he just administered a few brief swats with his paddle and was done. Just enough pain to ensure I received the message.

The room became very clear. I stopped kicking. I stopped yelling. The paddle went away. He stood me up and set a steady hand on my shoulder.

Now I understood who the boss was, and it was not me.

"You will be fine," he said. "Let us go meet your teacher."

The classroom smelled of crayons and paste. Sun fell across a low table set with paper and fat brushes. Kids murmured. Some watched me with wide eyes. The teacher, a woman with calm hands and a warm face, crouched until we were level.

"Good morning," she said. "I am glad you are here. Your spot is right there."

I sniffed and nodded. The principal guided me to a small chair, patted the back, and left. I did not cry. The memory of wood on skin kept me silent.

Minutes passed. I looked around. A boy next to me had a lunchbox with rockets. A girl across the table had ribboned braids and a smile that made my shoulders drop a notch. The teacher read a short story in a clear voice. We went outside to a small yard where the air smelled like damp dirt and chalk dust. The swing chains felt cool in my hands.

Back inside, the teacher rolled out finger paints. The room tilted toward joy. She tore big sheets of paper from a pad and set them in front of us. "Use the whole page," she said. "See what happens."

I pressed my fingers into a tray of red paint. It was cool and slick. The first smear ran across the paper like a sunrise. Blue followed, then a half-moon of yellow. I made shapes that looked like nothing and felt like everything. No one scolded me for the mess. The teacher smiled at the swirls and asked what I saw. My words came back on their own.

Out in the hall, a bell rang like a small metal bird. We lay on the carpet at rest time and looked at the ceiling tiles while the lights dimmed. I stared at the tiny holes and made constellations.

At pickup, my mother's face carried worry and guilt in equal parts. She searched for damage through the windows. She found me at the art table with both hands dipped to the wrists, showing two other kids how to drag a line of green into a line of blue and make a third color appear. I laughed. I did not want to leave. The principal arrived and escorted us to the front door.

"He's been such a great kid," he said to my mom. "You should be proud. He got along with all the other students, caused no trouble."

On the ride home, I held my painting flat on my knees and watched the wet shine wobble with each bump. The day started with panic and a paddle and ended with color on my hands and a story and a nap on a warm rug. The room had rules I could learn. The teacher's voice made the rules make sense.

That evening Mom wrote in my baby book in her loopy hand:

"I had a lot of fun. We didn't do anything. She read us a story, we played outdoors. We lay on the floor and rested. I was real brave and didn't cry."

The truth was simpler. I cried. The principal made sure I stopped. Then, an excellent teacher made sure I wanted to stay. I walked out with paint on my fingers and a new map in my head.

In those early school years, my teachers, principals, and administrators became safe adults. At least I knew people who seemed to respect me and treated me well.

That didn't last long.

Seccombe Lake

Seccombe Lake sat like a shallow U of light in the middle of San Bernardino, with concrete banks, a path that hugged the water, park benches warmed by the sun. The first time I saw it, I felt the click of a map in my head. Small, simple, knowable. A place I could learn.

We went often. Saturdays mostly. The car smelled of vinyl and sun. I carried my little rod and a tackle box that rattled when I walked.

At the water, the air changed. Warm, with a faint algae sweetness, a hint of metal from the benches. Ducks chattered. Dragonflies stitched the air, blue and green and copper, their wings buzzing like tiny machines. I knelt by the edge where the water was only a few inches deep and lifted a flat rock. An entire universe wriggled underneath. Water

27

boatmen skated. Mosquito larvae jerked like commas. Little snails grazed on slime that looked like nothing and fed everything. I watched until my knees ached, and my calves went numb, and then I watched longer.

"Pick a spot," Dad said, scanning the shore with a practiced eye. He carried the chairs, one in each hand, and set them with a precise two-foot gap that became the distance between us on good days.

We walked along the path. Sunflowers taller than me leaned over the rail. Milkweed pods fuzzed the air. Purple flowers grew out of cracks where they had no right to live. The path broke into little trails where kids had pushed through. Each one called my name.

"There," he said, pointing to a stretch where reeds framed a pocket of open water. "Fish like edges."

We sat. He opened the tackle box with little ceremony, the latches popping, a smell of metal and old water rising. He lifted a tiny bottle with orange eggs rolling inside.

"Gentle," he said, balancing one against my hook. "Let the point show just a little."

He baited his own and nodded toward the lake. His face was calm. The chores and the rules and the hard lines were somewhere else. Here, the rules belonged to the water and the line and the waiting.

We cast. The floats bumped, settled, and the ripples moved out in perfect circles that touched the reeds and came back thinner. The sun warmed my neck. A breeze pushed the path-side weeds into a slow bow. Time stretched. My breath matched the little lap of the water on concrete.

A tap. Then another.

"Now," he said.

I lifted. The line went tight, and the rod tip danced. A bluegill the size of my palm spun in the air, silver and green, a small, furious jewel. My heart climbed into my throat and stayed there. He grinned, a quick flash that made him look ten years younger.

"Good," he said. "Back she goes."

We slid the fish into the water. It vanished like a coin dropped into a fountain.

Sometimes Mom and my sister came. Mom read on a bench and laughed at the ducks, who begged like dogs. My sister fed them against instructions, and I watched their orange bills pinch bread with neat precision. Most days it was just me and Dad, chairs, lines, and silence. Dad rarely said anything, keeping his thoughts to himself.

Before the lake, we sometimes stopped at the tackle shop. The bell over the door gave a tired ring, and the room smelled like linseed oil, rubber boots, and dust. Pegboards held lures that looked like the drawer of a magician: feathers, bright spoons, tiny red and white floats, wiggly things that promised more than they ever delivered. I ran my finger over a row of sinkers, cold and dense as pebbles from another planet. Dad checked prices and held up what we could afford. He taught me names. Split shot. Crappie jig. Spoon. Words that fit in the mouth like good tools fit in the hand.

Back at the lake, I learned to see. The path around the U held pockets of difference: shade under a willow where the water cooled and minnows held still; a sunlit corner where dragonflies policed the air; a muddy inlet where frogs sang from the throat. I lifted rocks and put them back exactly where they came from. The world under each was complete. Tadpoles with tails that would become legs. Larvae that would become mosquitoes and feed the swallows that curved over the water at dusk. Everything belonged to everything else.

"Watch the line," Dad said without looking away from his float. "You'll see the bite before you feel it."

I watched. I learned to notice the tiny shift that meant tug, the tension that meant weed, the slow sideways slide that meant fish. The noticing bled into everything else. Where the reeds were thick, little fish hid. Where ducks gathered, food was near. Where the water darkened without wind, something moved below.

Geese flew into the lake now and then. I couldn't look at them, and they made my heart flutter every time I saw them.

We packed up when the heat went flat, and the shadows lengthened across the path. Chairs folded with a metal sigh. The tackle box snapped shut with the small satisfaction of something done right. In the car, the coins in my pocket chimed with each bump because I had remembered to take out the trash before we left. Cause and effect lined up. The day made sense.

On the ride home, I thought about the worlds under the rocks. How you could miss them if you did not kneel. How complete systems worked without anyone naming them. At night I lay in bed and pictured the lake path as a loop of choices: cast here or there, wait or move, pull or let it be. The loop repeated until it felt like a rule I could carry.

Years later, when life turned loud and complicated, that lake taught me what to look for. Edges where the action happened. Small signs that meant big changes coming. The truth that tiny, ignored things supported everything people noticed. It was a lesson in cooperation and in humility. If I moved one rock, I put it back. If I took a fish, I learned its name and weight and why it lived where it did.

I loved that little lake. Not because it was grand, but because it was small enough to understand and alive enough never to be boring. It taught me to map a place, to wait for the right moment, to see that every part touches every other part. It taught me that wonder hides in plain sight and that if you pay attention, a complete universe will open under a single stone.

The Closet

I was six years old, home on a Saturday afternoon while my mother ran errands. The house felt different when she was gone, bigger, quieter, full of shadows that stretched longer than they should. I wandered into my parents' bedroom, drawn by the mysterious adult world that was usually off-limits.

Their closet was a cave of treasures. I loved playing dress-up there, turning myself into distinct characters. That day I coated my face with my mother's bright red lipstick, the waxy smell filling my nose as I painted an exaggerated smile. I clomped in her high heels, leather straps loose around my small ankles, and dropped one of her big floppy hats over my eyes.

The closet smelled like them: her perfume sweet and flowery, his aftershave sharp and clean. Safety and danger tangled together, though I would not understand that contradiction for years.

Deep in the back, behind hanging clothes that brushed my face like curtains, I found a metal box. It was tucked away carefully, deliberately hidden. The metal was cold against my fingers. A small padlock held the secrets inside.

Maybe the box held secret treasures?

Six-year-old curiosity is a powerful force. I rummaged until I found something heavy, one of my father's shoes, I think, and smashed the lock. The metal gave with a satisfying snap. Inside, pictures lay scattered like secrets waiting to be discovered.

It was dark in the closet; I could not tell what the pictures showed. They felt important, forbidden in a way that made my stomach flutter with excitement and nerves. I was squinting, trying to make sense of shapes and shadows, when the closet door flew open.

"What the hell are you doing?"

My father filled the doorway, backlit by the bedroom light so his face was in shadow. I had never heard his voice like that, low and dangerous, like an animal warning you back.

"I was just playing," I said, my voice small. I dropped the pictures. They skittered across the floor like fallen leaves, some landing face up, others spinning into dark corners.

He stepped into the closet, and the air went thin. His presence pulled out the oxygen, the safety, the innocence that had been there seconds before.

"Those aren't for you," he said, voice controlled, deadly calm.

"I'm sorry, Daddy, I didn't know…"

His open hand connected with my face, the sound cracking off the closet walls like a gunshot. My head snapped sideways, stars bursting behind my eyes. Another slap. Then another. He was careful, always his palm, never his fist. Even in rage, calculating, making sure not to leave marks that would raise questions.

I was on the floor now, pictures beneath me, curling tight while he kept hitting me with those measured, stinging blows.

"You don't touch my things," he said between strikes. "You don't look at my things. You don't tell anyone about my things."

I tried to understand the anger. I had broken toys, dishes, even windows with baseballs and gotten in trouble, but nothing like this. This was different, bigger, like I had crossed an invisible line I did not know existed. Was it because the box was locked? Because the pictures were special? If I could figure out what I had done wrong, maybe I could fix it. Maybe he would stop.

The hitting did not stop. Then something worse started, something that made no sense, something my six-year-old brain had no way to understand. I decided this must be what happened to bad kids, terrible kids, though I could not think what I had done that was so terrible.

My dad forced me to watch in the mirror as he did terrible things to me. Those images still pop into my head, 60 years later.

When it was over, I was not the child who had been playing dress-up ten minutes earlier. The boy who entered that closet was gone.

That night changed everything. Before, I was a child growing up with a harsh father. I viewed him as a loving man who loved his children and wife, with occasional bursts of anger and a need to control.

After that, he was a monster.

But that was nothing compared to the change in him. I became different from a son; I was his property, an object. His emotions toward me slowly evolved into pure, white-hot hatred, more than I've ever observed in my life.

The Cover-Up

I stumbled out of that room crying, my face swollen and throbbing, blood on my shirt and shame burning through my chest like acid. Even through the confusion, part of my mind was already working, cataloging. The shame made no sense; I was the one who had been hurt, so I filed that contradiction for later.

My mother was at the stove, stirring a pot. The smell of dinner felt surreal after what I had just seen and what he had just done. This would be the test.

She looked up, took in the tears, the forming bruises, the way I held myself, then turned back to the burner without missing a beat.

"Go clean yourself up," she said, as casually as if I had come in from playing. "Dinner's almost ready."

So that's how this worked. Do not tell Mom about Dad.

"Mom, Daddy…"

"I said clean up, Richard." Sharp. Final. "And forget about it. It's not important."

She turned to look me directly in the eye, "Forget about it. Never happened."

"But…"

"Don't lie to me, young man."

"Mom," tears flowing from my eyes.

"Shut up." Then, in a commanding tone, "Forget about it. You hear me?"

"Yes, mom." Agreeing but not understanding.

I got it. I was not supposed to talk about it. I was supposed to pretend it did not happen. The message was obvious, even if I did not have words for it yet.

After dinner, after we all performed normally at the table while my face pulsed, I heard them down the hall, voices low. I could not make out the words, but the tone was obvious: negotiating the official version. Building a cover story.

Later I curled into the space under a desk behind a chair and let the emotions run while a separate part of my mind worked through what I had learned. Where had he been standing when he snapped? What did his voice sound like in the second before he moved? I replayed not only the blows but the lead-up: the shift in his footsteps, the tone that meant danger. My brain was already building a threat-assessment protocol.

The grown-ups were acting like nothing had happened, but something had happened, two things, in fact. The box in the closet had been filled with images of him with children. And then there was what followed. The rules in our house were not the rules I had been taught to expect.

I needed to be careful about where I went and what I touched. I needed to track his voice and how he moved. I needed to learn how to stay out of his path.

The fear, confusion, and hurt were still there, but they slid behind a new, colder awareness, a survival system that prioritized gathering information over processing feelings.

I was learning to watch instead of just experience, to analyze instead of react. That skill, born in terror and necessity, would reshape how my brain worked.

And then, for the most part, except for the occasional nightmare or flashback, I did forget. It was that or go insane.

The New Rules

The betrayal was complete. This was my father, the man who was supposed to protect me from monsters, not become one. He was my hero, the one I ran to when I was scared or hurt. Until that day, I would have trusted him with anything. I thought fathers kept their children safe.

Now I could not trust him with my own body.

I kept searching for a mistake that would make it make sense. Good dads did not do this. Right? My dad was good, everyone said so. He went to church, prayed before dinner, smiled and shook hands with neighbors. People respected him. There had to be an explanation.

There was not. There was only the truth: the person I trusted most decided I was worth less than his secret. Disposable.

In that dark closet, something fundamental shifted. If I could not trust my father, I could not trust anyone. If my mother could look at my bruised face and tell me to clean up for dinner, then I lived in a system where I needed to be entirely self-reliant.

This was not just devastation. It was clarity. The family's actual rules were visible now, and I could adapt.

It planted the seed of distrust that defined my relationship with my parents for the rest of their lives. I never let my guard down near my father again. Every interaction became a careful dance of observation, measuring his moods, reading warning signs, staying ready to avoid his space when danger appeared.

My distrust expanded over the years. I found it difficult to trust anyone, man or woman, but in different ways. As an adult, I continually braced for catastrophe. Anything good, in my mind, would soon be followed by horror.

Eventually, I concluded people were the problem, and this realization was to have profound effects on my life.

I learned to keep quiet so I could hear if he approached.

In open places, such as my room, I didn't play the radio, didn't listen to music, and faced the door whenever possible.

It was not only fear. My brain was building something more sophisticated: a pattern-recognition system to predict explosions before they happened. I tracked the shifts in his voice, the set of his shoulders, the particular silence that meant disappear. Over the next decade, I became a student of micro-expressions and atmospheric change.

The easy, trusting love children are supposed to feel for their fathers was gone, replaced by a watchfulness that would exhaust me for decades. It was also the beginning of the analytic skills that would make me exceptional at reading people and situations.

And my mother. I learned her protection came with conditions; her love secondary to her need for peace. I could no longer believe she would choose my safety over her comfort. So, I learned her patterns too, when she would dismiss problems, when raising hard truths would only make it worse.

I buried that memory so deep it took decades of therapy to dig it up. My mother confirmed it sideways over the years, dropping hints that eventually formed the full picture.

That day, my innocence did not just vanish. It was surgically removed, cut away with the same precision as the doctors who replaced my blood the day I was born.

What I could not know then—what took forty years to see—was that this was not only destruction. It was the start of a rebuilding project. When you learn at six that emotions are dangerous, that crying brings violence, that trust invites betrayal, that seeking comfort leads to abandonment, your brain gets creative about survival.

Mine chose analysis over feeling, patterns over people, systems over spontaneity. I became a child who could sit perfectly still through complex thoughts, who could watch other people's pain without being swept away by empathy, who could focus on projects for hours without noticing hunger, thirst, or the need for connection.

These were not deficits, though it took me decades to learn that. They were adaptations. Superpowers born of necessity. The same emotional distance that made me feel broken in relationships later let me edit another person's writing with ruthless objectivity. The intense focus that worried teachers became my greatest asset as a leader, programmer, designer, writer, and ghostwriter, letting me focus hard on problems and disappear into other people's stories for hours. The pattern-spotting that kept me safe from my father helped me decode what businesses and clients needed, even when they could not say it.

The trauma that almost destroyed me eventually made me exceptional at what I do. I just did not understand the connection for a long time.

My symptoms became my life plan. I just did not know their names yet.

Prepared was not paranoid. It was survival.

Report cards arrived twice a year in a sealed envelope that smelled like the school office. I knew what was inside before I opened it. I had been calculating for weeks.

My father reviewed them the way he reviewed everything — methodically, silently, with the specific quality of attention that meant he was building a case. He went line by line. Any grade below what he expected wasn't a conversation. It was a sentencing. The belt didn't need much of a reason.

So I worked. Not because the work interested me. Because a bad grade meant consequences I couldn't afford. I kept my grades at B+, A- through grade school on nothing but fear.

That's not the same thing as learning. But I didn't know the difference yet.

By six I had a working map of the house — where the danger lived, how fast it moved, which rooms were safe for how long. By ten I had a working map of the world: don't trust what people say, watch what they do, keep a hand on the exit. I didn't know I was building a system. I just knew the alternative was worse. The crazy in our household was strong, and it was going to get worse.

Chapter 2: Systems Emerge

The Christmas Pattern

One Christmas season, after I found out there is no Santa Claus, Mom had asked me to make a list of things I wanted. She even gave me a budget to work with. I spent days researching every item, prioritizing by desire and probability, creating a masterpiece of consumer analysis.

Christmas morning arrived, and not one item from my list appeared under the tree.

"Mom," I said, holding up my carefully researched list, "none of this is what I asked for."

She set her jaw, color rising. "Well, Santa probably thought these were better choices for you."

"But you asked me to make a list. You gave me a budget. I did research. Why make a list if nobody's going to use it?"

Her smile went flat. "Because I said so." She turned back to the counter, the paper towel tearing a little harder than it needed to.

Dad chuckled from behind his coffee cup, that sound he made when he thought I was being naive. "Maybe Santa knows something you don't, kid." His eyes, however, held a glint that said, *don't push this.*

The lesson was clear: your efforts would be dismissed, your research ignored, your reasonable expectations treated like childish fantasy. The family's promises meant nothing.

But the joke was on them. The cardboard boxes the presents came in were better than any toy. My sister and I spent the entire day turning them into fortresses, staging elaborate battles, building castles, and creating worlds that made sense in ways the adult world never would.

Finding Words That Didn't Hurt

"We're going to the library," Mom announced, but she didn't explain what that meant. My stomach clenched with the familiar dread of being dragged somewhere unfamiliar. In our house, surprise destinations usually meant sitting quietly in uncomfortable chairs while adults handled mysterious business or being deposited somewhere boring while Mom ran errands.

The word "library" meant nothing to me–it could have been a doctor's office, a government building, or some other place where children were expected to be silent and invisible. I dragged my feet getting ready, imagining another afternoon of staring at beige walls and trying not to fidget while grown-ups did grown-up things I wasn't allowed to understand.

Mom had to drag me from the car into the block building. Once we were inside, though, I was stunned into silence. Treasure!

The library smelled of old paper and possibility. Shelves stretched from floor to ceiling, packed with more books than I'd imagined existed in the entire world. My feet carried me down the aisles without permission, my eyes trying to absorb every title, every cover, every promise of worlds beyond our chaotic household.

The librarian greeted me as I went through the door, but I was pulling hard on Mom's arm, trying to get back to the safety of the car. This was all too new, too overwhelming. I didn't know the rules here, and at home, being in unfamiliar places usually meant trouble. But once I stopped fighting and looked around, I was stunned into silence. Treasure!

She materialized beside me in the science section, her sweater soft and smelling like lavender soap. She was probably in her sixties, with kind eyes behind wire-rimmed glasses and the patient demeanor of someone who genuinely enjoyed helping children discover books.

But I froze when she approached again. I didn't know the rules here. May I touch the books? Was I supposed to ask permission? I stood paralyzed between the shelves, my hands at my sides, afraid to reach for anything. The books were right there, calling to me, but what if I wasn't supposed to take them down?

She must have seen my hesitation because she put her finger to her mouth and "shushed" me gently, then picked me up and put me on the counter. Instead of scolding me for not knowing what to do, she reached into a drawer and pulled out a cookie.

"Finding anything interesting?" She asked, watching me stare at the endless rows of books while I nibbled the cookie uncertainly.

"Everything," I said, and meant it.

She helped me sort through my selections, her fingers gentle as she separated the possible from the impossible.

"How about we start here," she said, handing me a sheet covered with ten little spider drawings. "For every book you finish, you get a stamp. Fill up the sheet, and you get cookies and a new sheet."

"Really? I get rewarded for reading?"

"That's exactly right."

The spider stamps became my lifeline. Each book that I read meant another stamp, another step closer to cookies and validation. I burned through sheets like they were kindling, desperate for proof that someone valued what I loved doing anyway.

The weekly library trips became the highlight of my existence. Ten books at a time, the maximum allowed, each one a potential escape hatch from the constant psychological warfare at home. While my parents argued about money and mysterious adult grievances, I disappeared into stories where problems had solutions and heroes saved people. Worlds that made sense.

Time worked differently in the library. I'd sit on the floor between the stacks, completely absorbed, and suddenly realize hours had passed without my noticing. The same intensity that made sitting still in school feel like torture became a superpower when applied to things that interested me.

At Stater Brothers grocery store, I discovered another hiding spot on the bottom shelf of the magazine rack. Ballantine war books lined up like soldiers, each cover promising stories where strategy mattered and courage could overcome impossible odds.

I memorized battle formations the way other kids memorized baseball statistics. The German Panzer divisions, the Allied landing at Normandy, the tactics that worked and the ones that failed spectacularly. Military strategy made sense in ways that family dynamics never would–you could understand why things happened.

These weren't just adventure stories to me. They were proof that chaos could be beaten, that impossible problems had solutions if you could think clearly enough. The commanders in these books faced situations that seemed hopeless but found ways through them. That gave me something I desperately needed: hope that confusion and violence weren't permanent conditions.

The Battle of Iwo Jima book (after I discovered the history section of the library) was my first attempt at genuine adult material. College-level reading, but I was determined enough to push through it. When I finished that book, I felt like I'd accomplished something real. Not because it was difficult, but because it proved I could handle complexity when I needed to.

Art's Bookstore in downtown San Bernardino was a maze of narrow aisles and towering shelves; every surface covered with books that smelled like vanilla and dust. The science fiction section called me like a magnet, filled with rockets and aliens and futures that sparkled with possibility.

"Can I get this one?" I'd ask Mom, holding up Fantasy and Science Fiction magazine like it contained the secrets of the universe.

"I suppose," she'd say, probably wondering why her seven-year-old preferred spaceships to toy cars.

Jack Vance became my drug of choice. His alien worlds (especially a story called *Narrow Land*) were so completely different from San Bernardino that they might as well have been real. Better than real–they were places where logic and beauty could coexist, where problems had solutions if you were smart enough to find them.

When my grand aunt died and her belongings filled our living room in cardboard boxes, I claimed *Stranger in a Strange Land* like I was grabbing a life preserver. Heinlein's weird story about a Martian-raised human made perfect sense to me. Here was someone else who didn't understand the rules, who had to learn human behavior from the outside.

I read it twelve times until the pages were soft as cloth and the spine was held together with tape.

Building Something Real

But reading was passive. I was consuming other people's stories, other people's solutions, and other people's worlds where things made sense. I needed something I could create with my hands, something that would last, something that proved I could create order instead of just reading about it.

Barry's garage showed me what was possible. He was two years older, infinitely cooler, and owner of the most incredible display I'd ever seen–a sheet of plywood covered with hundreds of painted military miniatures. Tanks, trucks, soldiers, aircraft, all arranged in perfect formations that told stories without words.

"How long did this take?" I asked, my fingers hovering over the tiny figures.

"About two years," Barry said proudly. "Each one takes hours to get right."

The detail was incredible. Individual faces painted on soldiers the size of my thumbnail. This wasn't just playing with toys–this was creating entire worlds that made sense.

I knew instantly that I needed my own collection.

All the Christmas toys I'd been ignoring became currency. I sold them to neighborhood kids at bargain prices, converting plastic disappointments into cash for glue, paint, and my first model kits. The hobby gave me a legitimate reason to disappear from the household warfare while building something that operated according to rules I could understand.

The same intensity that let me read for hours now focused on painting details smaller than fingernails. Each model became a complete world I could control, where patience was rewarded and mistakes could be fixed. Barry and I spent entire afternoons in his garage, painting microscopic insignia, arguing about the relative merits of different tank designs, completely absorbed in miniature worlds that made sense in ways our real world never did.

When my parents added onto the house and I inherited the larger room, Dad helped me set up a model railroad (a

Christmas present) on a piece of plywood. It was one of our rare successful collaborations, his artistic eye and my obsessive attention to detail creating something genuinely impressive.

I spent months building plaster mountains, painting landscapes, laying track with precision that seemed important even though I couldn't explain why. Each tree was individually placed, each building carefully weathered to look authentic, each detail perfected even though no one else would notice or care.

My friends and I staged epic tank battles across this landscape, spending entire days maneuvering tiny armies through scenarios we'd read about in history books. The rest of the world disappeared during these sessions–no parents arguing, no school stress, no confusion about social rules I couldn't understand.

I was also constructing proof that chaos could be organized, that complex problems had solutions, that careful attention to detail produced results you could count on. Each completed project was evidence that I wasn't helpless, that I could make things work the way they were supposed to work.

More importantly, every minute I spent engrossed in building and painting models was a minute of peace from the constant family arguments. I faded into the background, introverted myself, and the parents briefly forgot I existed.

That meant freedom from Dad's belt and from Mom's manipulations. Freedom from their orders. Safety from Dad's yelling.

Working on my new hobbies, combined with reading, became my islands of safety. This began the process of introversion, something that would become my model of living for the rest of my life.

The Search for Order Amid Chaos

Time worked differently when I was focused on projects that mattered. Eight hours felt like twenty minutes. I'd start painting a model after breakfast and suddenly realize it was dinnertime, the entire day absorbed in the meditative process of applying tiny details that somehow felt enormously important.

This ability to disappear into sustained concentration was emerging as my secret weapon, though I did not know how valuable it would become. I could read an entire book in one sitting, memorize complex information effortlessly, maintain focus on tasks that interested me far longer than seemed humanly possible.

School remained a mystery of scattered attention and impossible boredom. Five minutes of math homework felt longer than five hours of model building. The disconnect was so complete it might as well have involved different species.

I discovered stamp collecting at the five-and-dime store, where a one-pound bag of stamps still stuck to envelope fragments cost just a dollar. Sorting through those random stamps, organizing them by country and theme, felt like archaeology. Each one told a story about places I'd never been, events I'd never heard of.

But the real treasure was a set of stamps from Tonga–completely unlike anything I'd seen before.

"These are amazing," I told the store clerk, holding up the circular stamps that felt strange and wonderful in my hands.

"Never seen anything like them," he agreed. "They're made of different materials–some are vinyl, some are metal foil. All self-stick too."

The Tonga stamps became an obsession. Their unusual shapes, materials, and designs appealed to something in my brain that craved systems with their own internal logic. I systematically collected the complete set, each new stamp a piece of a puzzle I was determined to finish. The Tonga collection, now complete except for a few super high-value issues, is one of the few that remains with me today.

Kenmore Stamps changed everything with its approval system. Sets would arrive in brown envelopes, and I'd spread them out on my desk like a jeweler examining stones. Keep the good ones; send back the rest. No pressure, no buyer's remorse.

"Another stamp package?" Mom would ask, watching me tear open the latest envelope.

"Only paying for the good ones," I'd explain, already sorting the keepers from the rejects with the analytical precision I brought to everything.

Each stamp had to earn its place in my collection. I'd evaluate condition, rarity, visual appeal, and how well it fit with stamps I already owned. The systematic approach to collecting was teaching me to make decisions based on objective criteria rather than impulse.

Comic books became another systematic obsession. This was back when they meant something–Marvel and DC were creating universes that operated on consistent rules, characters that developed over time, stories that built on each other in ways that rewarded careful attention.

I read everything. Spider-Man, Batman, X-Men, The Fantastic Four, Superman, The Avengers, The Justice League–every title I could get my hands on. By high school, I'd accumulated thousands of comic books, each one carefully bagged and catalogued, organized in ways that made sense to my systematizing brain.

"You've got more comics than some stores," David, my best friend, observed one day, looking at the towers of carefully organized issues in my room.

"I like complete sets," I said, which was true but didn't capture the deeper compulsion. I needed to understand entire fictional universes, to see how all the pieces fit together, to track character development across dozens of interconnected storylines.

That collection followed me when I moved out, boxes of carefully preserved comics that represented years of methodical collecting. I'd assumed they'd gained value over time–wasn't that how collectibles worked? When I finally decided to sell a few, I loaded a box into my car and drove to the local comic book store with high expectations.

"I'll give you a nickel each," the owner said after barely glancing through the box.

The words hit me like a physical blow. A nickel each. For comics I'd paid thirty-five cents for originally, that I'd protected in plastic bags, that represented countless hours of reading and organizing.

"That's it?" I asked, hoping I'd misunderstood.

He shrugged. "Unless they're key issues or really old, that's the market."

I drove home in stunned silence. That day, the entire collection (minus a few dozen that I knew were valuable) wound up in the trash bin. Thousands of comics, years of careful collecting, all worthless. It was my first lesson in the difference between personal value and market value–and how devastating that gap could be when you discovered it too late.

Drawing the World I Wanted

I started making pictures on paper–complex drawings that filled entire sheets with intricate designs. My bedroom floor was covered with detailed sketches that made sense only to me, elaborate charts that tracked relationships between ideas, and mechanical drawings of imaginary machines.

"What's all this?" Mom asked one day, looking at the papers spread across my desk.

"Just… drawings," I said, unable to explain that they were maps of how I thought the world should work.

The spaceship consumed dozens of sheets of paper as I worked out every detail. Engine systems, life support, navigation, crew quarters–each component drawn with technical precision, showing exactly how it would connect to everything else. I'd spend hours figuring out how the power would flow, where the fuel would be stored, and how the crew would move between sections.

These weren't random doodles. They were technical diagrams showing how systems could operate logically, how problems could be solved through proper engineering, how all the pieces could fit together if someone just designed things correctly. I was drawing blueprints for a universe that made sense.

The drawings became more sophisticated over time. Complex flowcharts showing decision trees, mechanical schematics for devices that could solve household problems, architectural plans for buildings where families could live without constant warfare. Each drawing was an attempt to impose order on chaos through systematic thinking.

But watching Dad with his art supplies, seeing how his creative intensity could coexist with such destructive behavior, poisoned the entire enterprise for me. How could I trust any form of expression that he had mastered? If someone capable of such cruelty could create beauty, then maybe the act of creation itself was compromised.

I made a decision that would shape the rest of my childhood: I would not be anything that my dad was. The logic was brutal but simple—if he did it, I wouldn't.

He smoked, so I never touched cigarettes. He drank, so alcohol became off-limits.

He had served in the military, so I would never join.

And he painted, so I abandoned art completely.

This wasn't just giving up a hobby. I was systematically rejecting entire categories of human experience because they belonged to him. I was willing to cut off parts of myself rather than risk becoming anything like the man who had hurt me. The fear of turning into him was so powerful that I'd rather live with less than risk inheriting his capacity for violence.

I abandoned drawing completely, packing up my supplies and diagrams like I was dismantling evidence of some shameful obsession. Art belonged to him now, tainted by his contradictions, and unusable as a refuge. I was choosing a smaller life if it meant a safer one—and at eight years old, that felt like the only rational response to an irrational situation.

The Shoplifting Lesson

The Sage's department store toy section was filled with plastic instruments that caught the fluorescent lights and threw rainbows across my vision. My fingers traced the smooth surfaces, imagining the music they could make. Dad stood three aisles over, examining painting supplies with that intense focus he brought to everything.

The instruments fit perfectly under my shirt, smooth and cool against my skin. I rejoined my parents, whistling innocently while my heart hammered with excitement and terror.

Dad's eyes found the bulges in my shirt before we even reached the car. His expression shifted from distraction to anger to something I couldn't read.

"We're going back inside," he said.

The store manager had kind eyes behind wire-rimmed glasses, but when Dad explained the situation, his expression grew serious.

"Son," the manager said, crouching down to my eye level, "do you know what happens to people who steal?"

My mouth went dry. "No, sir."

"They go to jail. Prison. Is that where you want to go?"

The image of iron bars and concrete cells filled my mind. "No, sir. Please don't call the police."

"If you promise me you'll never steal again, we can make this right. But if you're ever caught shoplifting again, anywhere, you will go to jail. Do you understand?"

"Yes, sir. I promise. I'll never steal again."

And I never did. That conversation planted itself so deeply in my brain that even decades later, I'd feel phantom handcuffs when walking past store security.

Dad handled it perfectly—clear consequences, logical progression, a lesson that stuck without violence or shame.

It was one of the few times his parenting actually made sense.

Body Stress Responses

The stomach aches always hit around midnight, when the house finally went quiet and my nervous system had time to process the day's accumulated tension. It felt like someone was twisting a knife in my gut, the pain so sharp it doubled me over.

"Mom," I'd whisper, padding down the hallway to their bedroom. "My stomach hurts really bad."

"It's probably something you ate," she'd mumble without opening her eyes. "Go back to bed."

But the pain would get worse, not better, until I was curled in a ball on the bathroom floor, sweating and nauseated. That's when they finally drove me to the emergency room at Kaiser Hospital.

The ER smelled of disinfectants and fear, fluorescent lights buzzing overhead while doctors in white coats poked and prodded my abdomen.

"Any tenderness here?" Dr. Martinez would ask, pressing various spots on my belly.

"Everything hurts," I'd say, though I couldn't explain why.

Blood tests, X-rays, urine samples–they ran every test they could think of, but the results always came back normal.

"Probably just stress," Dr. Martinez would conclude, his voice carrying the dismissive tone adults used when they couldn't fix something. "Kids his age don't usually have stress-related symptoms, but…"

He'd trail off, probably wondering what kind of household could stress a ten-year-old badly enough to send him to the ER with phantom stomach pain. Not just once, but at least a dozen times before.

The migraines were even worse. Pain that felt like an ice pick driving through my skull, starting behind my right eye and spreading like wildfire through my entire head. Light became torture, sound became unbearable, even the softest whisper felt like someone screaming directly into my brain.

"I can't see," I'd tell Mom, stumbling toward her voice with my eyes squeezed shut against the fluorescent kitchen lights.

"You're being dramatic," she'd say, not looking up from whatever she was cooking. "Take some aspirin and go lie down."

I lived on aspirin, buying those little metal tins at the drugstore every other day. The pharmacist started giving me worried looks when I appeared with my allowance money again.

"How many of these are you taking?" he asked one afternoon, watching me count out quarters for my third tin that week.

"Whatever it takes," I said, which was the truth but probably not the answer he was looking for.

The Hospital Lesson

The hospital exam room smelled like latex gloves and fear. The nurse was young, probably new, with kind eyes and a voice that suggested she actually cared about children.

"I need you to take off your shirt for the vaccine," she said gently.

I felt shy, exposed, so I just lifted my sleeve instead, hoping that would be enough.

"Take off your shirt," Dad said, his voice carrying that edge that meant non-negotiation.

When I hesitated, trying to work up the courage to expose myself to strangers, he reached over and literally tore the shirt off my back, fabric ripping as he yanked it over my head.

The nurse's face went white. Her eyes widened with horror, and I could see her processing what she'd just witnessed–the casual violence, the complete disregard for my dignity, the way my mother stood there watching without saying a word.

But like every other adult who witnessed Dad's behavior, she said nothing and did nothing. The system that was supposed to protect children apparently had rules about looking the other way.

I learned institutions would fail me when it mattered most. That lesson would prove valuable in ways I couldn't imagine.

Lola's Sanctuary

The one shining exception among adults was a woman named Lola. She was probably in her seventies, lived on the corner, and had turned her house into a botanical wonderland. Every surface was covered with plants, mostly cacti in amazing varieties.

She also had an incredible rock collection: petrified wood, onyx, quartz, specimens I'd never imagined existed. She and I would spend hours talking, and she was the only adult I considered a genuine friend during my entire childhood.

"Tell me about this one," I'd say, holding up a piece of turquoise.

"That's from Arizona," Lola would explain, settling into her chair like she had all day to share what she knew. "The Native Americans believed turquoise could protect travelers and bring good luck."

"Does it work?"

She'd smile. "Well, I'm still here, aren't I? And I've traveled all over the world."

Lola was the first adult who treated me like my questions mattered, who shared knowledge without condescension, who seemed genuinely interested in what I thought about things. Through her, I built my rock collection, learning about formations and mineral properties from someone who found wonder in the world instead of reasons to be angry.

Her house smelled like earth and growing things, completely different from the tension and chemical sharpness of home. I could sit for hours examining specimens, learning about how different stones formed over millions of years, absorbing knowledge about how the natural world worked.

"See these layers?" she'd say, pointing to bands in a piece of sandstone. "Each one represents thousands of years. You're looking at time itself."

Lola proved that some adults could be trusted, that knowledge could be shared without strings attached, that curiosity was something to be encouraged rather than punished. She was showing me what functional relationships looked like.

Belinda

From the day she was born, Belinda was my best friend. Not in the way children are told to get along — we actually liked each other. We played together, talked, invented elaborate games that made sense only to us. I showed her rocks and explained where they came from. I showed her insects and named them. She was curious about everything, and I was the person who knew things, which is a good arrangement between siblings.

She raised hamsters and mice. She watched everything carefully, kept notes in her head the way I kept them in mine. Later she became a scientist. I like to think I had something to do with that — not the formal education part, but the part where you decide the world is interesting enough to spend your life looking at it closely.

In a house where everything was either dangerous or indifferent, she was neither. She was just there, small and steady, the one relationship in my childhood that cost nothing and asked nothing and gave me something I didn't have a name for until much later: unconditional.

My Sister's Seizure

We were playing on the school playground during recess, something silly that had us both laughing until our sides hurt. She was in the middle of telling me a joke when her face suddenly went blank, like someone had flipped a switch inside her head.

That was one of the most terrifying things I've seen in my entire life.

"Belinda?" I said, but she wasn't responding. Her eyes rolled back until only the whites showed. She fell to the ground, and her whole body started shaking.

It wasn't like shivering from cold–this was violent, uncontrolled convulsions that made her arms and legs jerk like a broken marionette. Foam appeared at the corners of her mouth, and the sound she was making wasn't human.

"Help!" I screamed at the top of my lungs, my voice cracking with panic. "HELP! Something's wrong with my sister!"

Kids scattered in all directions while teachers came running from across the playground. The principal reached us first and immediately dropped to his knees beside her.

"It's okay," he said, his voice calm and professional while he gently placed a pencil between her teeth. "She's having a seizure. It looks scary, but she's going to be fine."

"Is she dying?" I asked, tears streaming down my face as I watched her body continue its terrible dance. To hell with Dad and his "men don't cry"; this was my sister!

"No, son. Just stay back and let me help her."

When the convulsions finally stopped, she lay there unconscious, breathing heavily but peacefully. The playground had gone completely silent except for her labored breathing and my sniffling.

Later, when my grandparents heard about the episode, they had their own diagnosis.

"She's possessed by demons," Grandmother announced with absolute certainty. "That child needs an exorcism, not doctors."

"Mother," my mom said, exhaustion heavy in her voice, "she has epilepsy. It's a medical condition."

"Don't you sass me, young lady. I know evil when I see it. All that thrashing and foaming at the mouth–that's the devil trying to claim her soul."

Fortunately, my parents ignored the demonic possession theory and got her actual medical treatment. But I'd learned something important about family wisdom: sometimes the people who claimed to love you most had the worst possible advice.

Cats vs. Scruffy

The cats were my most reliable companions, though I've forgotten their names over the decades. What I remember is their weight on my lap when the house was too loud or too quiet, their purring that vibrated through my chest like a healing frequency. They never judged me for being weird, never promised things they couldn't deliver, never turned affection into a weapon.

When I was crying in my closet refuge after one of Dad's explosions, they'd find me and curl up against my side, their warm bodies a reminder that someone in this house cared about my wellbeing, even if it was just an affectionate cat.

Scruffy was everything the cats weren't–aggressive, unpredictable, constantly angry at the world. He was a medium-sized mutt with matted fur and eyes that held nothing but suspicion and rage.

"Here, Scruffy," I'd say, offering him a treat and keeping my voice gentle. "Good boy."

Without warning, his teeth would sink into my hand, drawing blood and leaving puncture wounds that took weeks to heal.

"What did you do to provoke him?" Dad would ask, examining my latest bite marks with accusatory eyes.

"Nothing! I was just trying to be nice to him."

"Dogs don't bite for no reason. You must have done something."

But Scruffy's most bizarre obsession was with mail delivery. Every day around eleven, he'd position himself by the front door like a furry sentry, waiting for the mailman's approach.

The moment letters started sliding through the slot, Scruffy would explode into action, grabbing envelopes in his teeth and shaking them like they were mortal enemies. Bills,

Christmas cards, letters from relatives–nothing survived his daily assault on the postal service.

"Scruffy, no!" Mom would shout, trying to rescue what remained of our correspondence.

But he'd already reduced the day's mail to confetti, pieces of important documents scattered across the entryway like the aftermath of a paper shredder explosion.

The mailman probably dreaded our house more than any other stop on his route, never knowing if today would be the day Scruffy figured out how to open the door and take their feud to the next level.

Field Trips

Something that I enjoyed most of my life is the simple act of getting out of an enclosed space. Sitting in a small room listening to a teacher drone on or reading some boring material was never my idea of fun. I've learned my most useful lessons from visits to the great outdoors, seeing what man and nature have accomplished.

My elementary school teachers enjoyed taking all their students out on field trips. These little one-day trips were great, as they were a chance to get out of the stuffy classroom to see the real world. We went on maybe two or three field trips a year.

"Field trip tomorrow!" Mrs. Henderson announced one Friday afternoon, and the entire classroom erupted. Kids bounced in their seats, papers rustling as everyone turned to whisper excitedly to their neighbors. My stomach did that familiar flip of anticipation mixed with anxiety–what if something went wrong? What if I got in trouble? But the excitement won out. Anything was better than another day trapped within these four walls.

Most commonly, the teacher would load us all onto a school bus, and we'd soon find ourselves in a nice field or some other nearby habitat. The bus ride itself was an adventure–the smell of vinyl seats mixing with twenty-seven different lunch bags, the rhythmic bouncing that made my teeth chatter, kids pressing their faces against windows steamed with breath.

"Look! There's a hawk!" someone would shout, and we'd all crane our necks to see a distant speck circling overhead.

For example, one teacher bused us all over to Little Mountain, which was a large hill on the other side of town. This hill was bare; not a single tree or house was on its flanks. It was covered with sagebrush, grass and shrubs.

The wind hit us the moment we stepped off the bus, carrying the sharp, clean smell of sage and dry grass. My shoes crunched on gravel and dried vegetation as we formed our ragged line, everyone talking at once until Mrs. Peterson raised her hand for silence.

"Stay together," she called out, her voice carrying across the open space. "And watch where you step!"

We'd then wander around with the teacher as she pointed out various elements of the landscape. "These are rabbit droppings," she'd say, crouching down to examine small, dark pellets scattered near a clump of brush. "And these are the bones of a large rodent, maybe a rat."

I knelt beside her, fascinated by the tiny white fragments. "How do you know it was a rat?" I asked.

"See the size of these teeth marks on this bone? Too big for a mouse, too small for a wolf or a big cat."

The sun beat down on the back of my neck, making me squint as I examined the evidence of invisible dramas playing out in this seemingly empty landscape.

While the trips to the outdoors were great, the trips that I remember the most are those to various manufacturing facilities. My favorite was when the teacher took us on a tour of the San Bernardino Sun-Telegram.

The building hit us with a wall of sound before we even got inside–the rumble and clatter of machinery, voices calling over the noise, the rhythmic thump-thump-thump of printing presses. The smell was intoxicating: ink, paper, metal, and something else I couldn't identify but would later learn was the hot metal of the linotype machines.

The Sun-Telegram was the newspaper for San Bernardino. The plant was located downtown, and seemed, to us, to be the hugest thing we children had ever seen in our lives. A portly, bearded man in ink-stained coveralls guided us through the entire operation.

"Welcome to where the news gets made!" he bellowed over the machinery, his voice booming with obvious pride. "How many of you read the paper at home?"

A few hands went up tentatively.

"Well, you're about to see how it all happens, from the very first word to the paper on your doorstep!"

We started at the beginning–by meeting some reporters. Our guide introduced us to a kindly old gentleman hunched over a typewriter, his fingers flying across the keys with impossible speed.

"This is Mr. Williams," our guide explained. "He's been covering the police beat for fifteen years. Mr. Williams, tell the kids what you do."

The reporter looked up, his eyes twinkling behind thick glasses. "I find out what happened, then I tell everyone about it. Simple as that." His fingers never stopped moving as he talked, the typewriter creating its own percussion section. "The trick is asking the right questions and listening to the answers."

Then we saw the rest of the operation. The linotype room was like stepping into another world–hot, loud, filled with the smell of molten metal. The operator, a thin man with rolled-up sleeves and sweat on his forehead, worked the keyboard while explaining the process.

"See, I type the story here," he said, his hands dancing over keys that looked nothing like a regular typewriter, "and the machine melts lead and creates these slugs of type." Hot metal hissed and bubbled in the crucible beside him.

We were awed by the linotype machine and were thrilled when the operator gave each a sample of the machine's product. The metal was still warm in my palm, the letters backwards but perfectly formed. I rubbed my thumb over the raised surface, amazed that these tiny metal pieces would soon become words thousands of people would read.

I still have that piece of linotype in my childhood collection.

We were amazed when we saw the tremendous printing presses and the huge rolls of paper. The press room was a cathedral of machinery–massive cylinders spinning at incredible speed, paper feeding through in an endless stream, the finished newspapers emerging folded and ready. The noise was overwhelming, a thunderous rhythm that I felt in my chest.

"How fast does it go?" I shouted to our guide.

"Thirty thousand papers an hour!" he shouted back, grinning at our wide-eyed expressions. "By tomorrow morning, half the city will be reading words that were just thoughts in Mr. Williams' head an hour ago!"

That was a great field trip! Walking back to the bus, my head was spinning with the complexity of it all–the chain of people and machines that turned events into news, thoughts into printed words that reached thousands of homes.

Another time, we went to a bottling plant–I think it was a Coca-Cola plant. The sweet smell hit us before we even entered the building, like walking into a candy store mixed with a machine shop. This was a fascinating experience for a young boy.

"Don't touch anything unless I say so," warned our guide, a woman in a white coat who had to speak loudly over the clatter of glass bottles moving through the machinery. "Everything here moves fast, and we can't stop the line."

I was amazed by everything from the bottle washers to the bottle fillers on the other end of the line. The bottles moved like an army of glass soldiers, marching in perfect formation through steaming jets of water, then emerging clean and gleaming under bright lights.

"Where do the dirty bottles come from?" asked Sarah, one of my classmates.

"People return them to stores," the guide explained. "We wash them, inspect them for cracks, then fill them again. Each bottle gets used dozens of times."

The filling station was hypnotic–bottles sliding into position, getting filled with exactly the right amount of dark, fizzy liquid, then moving on to get capped with a satisfying pop-hiss sound that repeated hundreds of times per minute.

"Can we taste it?" someone called out hopefully.

"After the tour," she promised, and we all exchanged excited glances.

On yet another field trip, the entire class visited the basement of the local Sages department store. This was fascinating in a completely different way–quieter, more organized, like discovering the hidden clockwork beneath a familiar surface.

The basement smelled like cardboard or fabric, a scent I'd never noticed before but would recognize forever. Our guide, a friendly man in a tie and vest, led us through narrow aisles between towering shelves.

"This is where all the magic happens," he said with a conspiratorial whisper. "Upstairs, customers see the finished store. Down here, we see how it all comes together."

We saw how they printed the signs–a small printing press churning out price tags and sale banners; the operator adjusting fonts and checking colors with the precision of an artist. We watched how the shelves were stocked–workers consulting detailed lists, checking item numbers, organizing merchandise with systematic efficiency that made me think of my model collections at home.

"How do you know where everything goes?" I asked, genuinely curious.

"Every item has a number," he explained, showing us a clipboard covered with codes. "Every shelf has a number. Match them up, and customers can find what they need."

The merchandise unloading area was like watching a carefully choreographed dance–trucks backing up to loading docks, workers moving boxes with dollies and hand trucks, everything sorted and labeled and directed to its proper destination.

After sixth grade, the field trips just… ended. Junior high and most of high school meant being trapped in classrooms, reading about the world instead of experiencing it. I didn't realize how much I'd miss those glimpses behind the scenes until they were gone.

But those elementary field trips gave me something crucial: proof that the world operated on logical systems that could be observed and understood. The newspaper had a clear process from reporters gathering information to printed papers rolling off massive presses. The bottling plant had elegant automation moving bottles through predictable stages. Even the department store basement revealed organized systems for managing inventory and signage.

These glimpses behind the scenes showed me that complex operations could run smoothly when people understood their roles and followed systematic procedures. The adults running these facilities knew what they were doing and could explain their work clearly to curious children. It was a sharp contrast to the emotional chaos at home, where nothing seemed to follow predictable rules.

I started paying attention to how things worked–not just what people said they did, but the observable processes that produced consistent results. The linotype operator didn't just talk about making type; he showed us the machine in action and gave us samples we could examine. The bottling plant supervisor didn't just describe the process; she walked us through each station so we could see bottles being washed, filled, and capped in perfect sequence.

These field trips became my first education in systems thinking, though I wouldn't have that vocabulary for years. I learned that complexity didn't have to mean chaos, that people could work together efficiently when they understood their purpose, and that the most interesting learning happened when you could observe actual processes rather than just read about them.

When the field trips stopped in junior high, I felt the loss acutely. School became just sitting in rooms listening to theories about how things worked instead of seeing actual systems in operation. I didn't realize it then, but those field trips planted the seeds for my eventual career in understanding how complex systems really function–and helping others decode the processes that produce results.

Runaway Attempt

Running away seemed like the logical solution when I turned eight. I packed my few precious belongings–some books, the most important rocks from collection, a change of clothes that smelled like our laundry soap.

"I'm running away to join the circus," I announced to Mom, expecting tears or attempts to talk me out of it.

Instead, she laughed and made me lunch. Even my escape attempt was treated like entertainment.

I walked down Stoddard Street to Hund's Market, then left for three blocks, right for four blocks, left again. The traffic light stood like a boundary between the world I knew and the world beyond. My little bag of belongings felt heavier with each step.

That's when the realization hit me like a physical blow: I was leaving my sister alone with him. Belinda. The one person in that house who was genuinely glad to see me, who followed me around wanting to know things, who kept her hamsters in careful cages and named every one of them. She was five years old and she had no idea what I protected her from, and if I left she would have no one.

No telling what Dad might do without me there to witness it, to intervene, to at least create the possibility of consequences. She was smaller than me, more vulnerable, less capable of fighting back or running away.

I turned around and retraced my exact route, arriving home before dinner, my escape attempt abandoned for her sake. Protection had become my primary responsibility, a weight that would shape every decision I made for years to come.

My parents relayed my attempt to each other at diner. They thought it was all a big joke.

It's a good thing I remained at home. I saw a certain look in Dad's eye, the way he held his posture, on more than one occasion. When that happened, I'd quietly pull my sister into my room to play a game or ask if she wanted to make cookies for us with her Easy-Bake oven. A few times, I stood between Dad and her when he became particularly threatening. I never told her what I was doing; it was almost too much for my brain to handle, but I made sure she was safe as much as possible.

Books didn't yell at me. Model kits didn't hit me. Rocks didn't change the rules without warning. These things were reliable in ways that people weren't.

The damage was becoming the skillset, one carefully constructed system at a time.

Order wasn't peace, but it kept the floor from tilting.

Chapter 3: Extended Family Toxicity

The Invisible Grandparents

My father's parents might as well have been fictional characters for all the impact they had on my life. Justin Vernon Lowe and Katherine Amanda Rumohr Lowe existed somewhere in the background of our family story, mentioned occasionally but never really present.

Justin had served 27 years in the U.S. Navy, rising from apprentice seaman in 1925 to chief warrant officer when he retired in 1954. Katherine had immigrated from Germany in 1914 at age six, arriving at Ellis Island just months before World War I began. They'd married in 1929 and stayed together for 43 years until Justin's death from lung cancer in 1972.

By any measure, they should have been significant figures in my life. They were my grandparents. They lived within driving distance. But they maintained such distance that I met my grandfather exactly twice in my life and have no memory of either occasion.

When Justin got sick in 1972, the entire experience became a perfect example of how children were treated in our family. Dad, Mom, my sister and I hurriedly packed and took off for Texas–specifically, Alamogordo. Twelve hundred miles over two days in a station wagon, with my parents arguing the entire way. Even grandfather's illness didn't bring any peace to their constant bickering.

After making that huge trip, putting up with the discomfort of driving across the country with squabbling parents, they didn't even let me see my grandfather. My parents decided that we "couldn't take the sight of him" with all the wires and equipment hooked up to him. They thought it would scare us, I guess.

I was 12 years old and perfectly capable of making my own decisions about what I could handle. But that didn't matter. Grandfather died a few days later. Dad rushed back out to Texas for the funeral while Mom, my sister, and I stayed home. No closure, no last goodbye, no acknowledgment that we might have wanted to pay our respects.

This wasn't accidental neglect. It resulted from a rigid household philosophy that children were unimportant and should be neither seen nor heard. From their perspective, children existed in a separate sphere from adult concerns.

There was one exception—a Christmas when both grandparents visited us in San Bernardino. They stayed at the Wigwam Village, where the rooms were concrete replicas of Indian teepees. I was fascinated by the teepee rooms and afterward became engrossed in learning about Native American culture for years.

We had a Christmas celebration, and the grandparents gave us presents. These were much easier visits than the chaos of Hoeffer Christmases—a big relief from all that drama.

But even their gift-giving revealed how disconnected they were from who we actually were. I remember getting what Grandmother called a "Mexican rattle"—basically a gourd with seeds in it. A bunch of socks that weren't anything I would wear. One of those Russian nesting dolls. The gifts were strange and seemed to be chosen by people who knew nothing about my interests or personality.

While the Hoeffer side of the family was actively toxic–full of manipulation, verbal abuse, and emotional warfare–the Lowe side was simply absent. Neither approach provided anything resembling a healthy family connection, but the contrast was telling. Active toxicity at least acknowledged that children existed. The Germanic approach treated children as fundamentally irrelevant to the adult world.

The Man Who Survived Everything

For most of my young life, the only things I knew about Grandfather Hoeffer were that he was in World War 2 and he loved to cook. He was the cook at every family event, and because of that, we'd pile into the car and drive down to grandmother's house for holiday meals.

The rest of the family warned me to avoid grandfather. They said he was cranky, a curmudgeon, and difficult to get along with. He'd snapped at me a few times during visits, but I was used to that by my parents, so it didn't bother me.

When I was 17, I decided it was time to learn more about my grandfather. Gathering up my courage, I approached him. He saw me coming and patted the chair next to him. Obviously, an invitation.

I sat down, and he told me his story.

The conversation lasted for hours. He spoke in the same methodical way he did everything else–precise details, exact dates, careful observations. But there was something different in his voice that day, a quality I'd never heard before. Relief, maybe. Or recognition that someone was finally asking the right questions.

What I learned that day was that my grandfather's experience went far beyond being "a cook in World War Two." He had survived three years and four months as a prisoner of war in Japanese camps–but his story began much earlier and revealed a character forged by principles that would never bend, even under the most extreme circumstances.

Before the war, he served as a ship's cook on the USS Oahu, part of the U.S. Navy Yangtze River Patrol stationed in Shanghai, China. Even then, his methodical nature was apparent–he kept detailed records of provisions, documented weather patterns, and maintained his kitchen with military precision. His shipmates later said he could make a decent meal from almost nothing, a skill that would become crucial to his survival.

His journey toward that long imprisonment started in November 1941 when the *USS Oahu* was ordered out of Shanghai as war tensions escalated. They arrived in Manila just days before Pearl Harbor was bombed. When the Philippines fell, he became one of the defenders of Corregidor–that fortress that held out for months against impossible odds. Even during the siege, when men were reduced to eating anything they could find, grandfather continued to organize the food distribution with mathematical fairness, ensuring that every man received the same portions regardless of rank or friendship.

The surrender came on May 6, 1942. Grandfather watched American and Filipino forces stack their weapons in neat piles, then begin the march that would become known as the Manila Death March–though his experience was slightly different as a naval prisoner. The forced march from the prison camps to transportation points, under brutal conditions with no food or water, was just the beginning of a program of dehumanization that would define the next three years of his life.

In 2025, I used his journal to write a memoir based on the time he spent from 1937 to 1945 as a Naval officer and a POW. It's called *Behind the Wire*, and is available for sale online.

What struck me most about his account was not just the brutality he endured, but how he maintained his essential character throughout. While other prisoners despaired or gave up hope, he maintained his role as observer and recorder. In his neat handwriting, he noted which guards were cruelest and which companies treated prisoners slightly better. He tracked the changing rations as the war turned against Japan—not just the quantities, but which prisoners were getting short measure and why. He documented the ingenious ways prisoners found to sabotage Japanese war production—overloading cargo nets until ship booms collapsed, dropping vital radio equipment "accidentally," hiding crucial parts from machinery bound for Manchuria.

His survival wasn't just about enduring—it was about active, calculated resistance. When assigned to dismantle the Voice of Freedom radio station in Malinta Tunnel, he and his fellow prisoners destroyed as much equipment as possible while appearing to cooperate. They cut wires short enough to be useless, broke expensive vacuum tubes by "accidentally" dropping them and removed vital connections that would take hours to discover. Every act of sabotage was planned meticulously and executed with the same precision he'd once used to manage a ship's galley.

But it was the smaller moments that revealed his character most clearly. The way he and other prisoners shared their meager rations with sick men, even when it meant going hungrier themselves. How he carefully documented the names and fates of fellow prisoners in tiny handwriting on scraps of paper he kept hidden in his shoes, understanding that someone needed to remember their stories, that their deaths needed to mean something beyond the casual brutality that claimed them. He recorded not just names but details–where they were from, what they'd hoped to do after the war, messages they wanted passed on to families they'd never see again.

That he never lost his sense of justice, even when surrounded by casual cruelty, amazed me. He would intervene when guards singled out weaker prisoners for special abuse, not through confrontation but through clever misdirection– spilling something that required cleanup, asking questions about work assignments, anything to break the guard's focus and give the victim a chance to disappear into the crowd. He organized informal tribunals among the prisoners to settle disputes fairly rather than letting desperation turn them against each other. When food went missing from someone's small hoard, Grandfather would investigate methodically until he found the truth, then broker solutions that preserved both justice and group cohesion.

The manuscript revealed the details in precise detail: starvation rations of 700 grams of rice and thin vegetable soup per day for men doing hard labor that should have required 3,000 calories.

The casual violence of guards who would beat prisoners for entertainment, or for breaking rules they'd never been told existed.

The "ten-man shooting squads" where if one prisoner escaped, all ten in his group would be executed–a policy that turned potential allies into desperate watchmen.

The sick prisoners relegated to what they called "the death house"–a former baseball stadium where men were left to die on half-rations with no medical care, their bodies stacked like cordwood each morning.

Through it all, grandfather maintained his routines. He woke at the same time each day, performed the same mental exercises, said the same silent prayers for his wife and daughter back home. He never stopped believing the war would end and that he would return to them. When other men gave up, he would sit with them and talk about what they would do when they got home, what meals they would eat, what jobs they might find. He made survival into a form of resistance–not just staying alive, but staying human in a system designed to reduce men to animal desperation.

His leadership was quiet but unmistakable. Prisoners came to him with problems not because he had any official authority, but because they trusted his judgment. When someone was caught stealing, grandfather would broker the consequences. When men planned sabotage, they asked his advice on timing and execution. When someone was dying, grandfather would sit with them through their final hours, making sure they weren't alone, sometimes writing down their last words for families he hoped someday to find.

The systematic nature of the brutality was what struck him most–this wasn't random cruelty but carefully calculated dehumanization. Prisoners were fed just enough to work, beaten just enough to break their spirit but not enough to prevent labor, given just enough hope to prevent mass suicide attempts, but never enough to sustain real resistance. The Japanese understood exactly how much abuse the human body and spirit could absorb while remaining functional. Grandfather's response was equally organized– he found ways to give men back their dignity in small doses, to maintain connections that the system tried to sever, to preserve knowledge and memory that the camps tried to erase.

When the war finally ended on August 16, 1945, grandfather weighed roughly half what he had when captured. His teeth were loose from malnutrition, his body was covered in scars from beatings and untreated injuries, and his hands shook from nerve damage that would never fully heal. But his mind remained sharp and his moral compass intact. While other prisoners wept or raged or stared in stunned disbelief at their liberation, grandfather methodically gathered the scraps of paper where he'd recorded the names and stories of men who hadn't survived. Those records would later help families learn the fate of loved ones who had simply disappeared into the Pacific theater.

The reunion at that bus station in Auburn was the collision of two entirely different wars–his specific horrors of brutality carefully endured and methodically resisted, and grandmother's diffuse trauma of endless uncertainty and single parenthood during wartime. She had spent years not knowing whether he was alive or dead, rationing hope the same way she rationed food. He had spent years knowing exactly what he faced each day but never knowing if tomorrow would bring liberation or death. They were both survivors, but of completely different kinds of hell.

That conversation changed everything between us. Where once I'd seen a cranky old man who occasionally barked at children, I now saw someone who had witnessed history's darkest chapters and somehow emerged intact. More than intact–he had emerged with his humanity strengthened, not diminished.

Out of all the family members, grandfather was the one I respected. Period. He was a bit strange–muttered to himself, made clicking noises with his teeth–but I figured he earned it. After what he'd been through, he could mutter and click all he wanted. The man who insisted on feeding everyone at family gatherings wasn't just being hospitable. He was performing an act of resistance against a world that had once tried to starve him.

The Bitter Victim

What I didn't learn much later was that grandfather's trials didn't end with liberation. He came home to face a different kind of daily assault from the person who should have been most grateful for his survival.

Grandmother Jeanette was a whiny, victim-focused person who filled their house with astrology magazines, UFO books, and Buddhist paraphernalia. While grandfather had earned his trauma through objective horror, grandmother seemed to have nursed hers from life's ordinary disappointments.

She had waited six years during the war, not knowing if her husband was alive or dead, raising my mother alone during wartime rationing and uncertainty. That experience could have forged strength and resilience. Instead, it seemed to have convinced her that life owed her something it hadn't delivered.

Her weapon of choice was verbal assault. She belittled grandfather constantly, turning his quiet dignity against him. She'd mock his methodical ways, dismiss his careful observations, and treat a man who had survived the unimaginable as though he were an incompetent child.

The house reflected her scattered worldview—stacks of publications about ancient astronauts, horoscopes, and mystical healing alongside dusty Buddhist statues and crystals. It felt like the physical manifestation of someone grasping at anything that might explain why life hadn't worked out the way she'd imagined.

Her bitterness was covert but constant. She'd make cutting remarks disguised as casual observations, deliver insults wrapped in concern, and create an atmosphere where everyone had to walk carefully to avoid triggering one of her wounded martyr performances.

I avoided her as much as possible. Even as a child, I could sense that her approach to life's difficulties was exactly what I didn't want to become.

Watching her attack grandfather was my first real lesson in how some people deal with their own inadequacy—they tear down anyone who shows them what actual strength looks like.

The Underminer

But Grandmother's whiny approach was transparent compared to what I witnessed from my aunt. If grandmother just wanted everyone to feel sorry for her, my aunt was something more dangerous—someone who actively worked to undermine people while maintaining a facade of concern.

She had learned from grandmother's example but refined it into something more calculated. She'd pile onto grandmother's criticisms of grandfather, but her attacks were subtle, delivered with fake concern and disguised as helpful observations. Where grandmother would openly complain about grandfather's "difficult" behavior, Pam would say things like, "Poor Dad, he just can't seem to adjust to normal life, can he?"

Her undermining was surgical. She'd plant seeds of doubt about people's competence, their motivations, their character—always framed as worry or disappointment rather than direct attack. She was the family member who would smile to your face while systematically destroying your reputation behind your back.

This came through clearly in an interview someone did with family members about their childhoods. Her responses revealed how she'd perfected this approach. When asked about grandmother, she said:

"She gives a lot. She's a real giving, loving person. Then there's the other price you pay for her doing it."

Notice how she sounded supportive while simultaneously planting the idea that grandmother was manipulative. Even when acknowledging dysfunction, she positioned herself as the wise observer who could see what others missed. About her parents' religious behavior, she complained:

"When I got to be sixteen, I realized what hypocrites they were."

But her grievances were always calculated to make her look like the most insightful person in the room while subtly undermining everyone else's credibility.

The interview revealed someone who could identify problems in others while presenting herself as the innocent victim of their dysfunction. She described her life as "pretty boring" while systematically painting every other family member as somehow deficient. When asked about her many failed marriages, she explained:

"You know sometimes you pull in the same people, more or less, even though they're not the same there are certain traits they seem to pull in with them. And he had the same traits as Marty. Irresponsibility."

She had enough self-awareness to recognize patterns but used that awareness to avoid responsibility while undermining others.

Years later, after grandfather's death from Alzheimer's, she would claim she had written his manuscript–the book I had actually ghostwritten from his handwritten notes and our long conversations. It was her classic move: take credit for meaningful work while subtly suggesting that the person who actually did it wasn't capable of such accomplishment.

After grandfather's death, she created an elaborate memorial website celebrating him as a beloved patriarch. The irony was staggering–the same person who had spent years undermining his dignity now played the grieving, devoted family member online. Anyone finding that website would see touching tributes to a cherished grandfather, with no hint that she had spent years subtly destroying his credibility at family gatherings.

This was what made her more dangerous than Grandmother. Grandmother's self-pity was obvious and could be avoided. My aunt's undermining was covert, designed to make you question your own perceptions while she maintained plausible deniability.

The One Who Escaped

There was another family member who stood apart from all this dysfunction. Uncle Frank, my mother's brother, had escaped. While everyone else remained trapped in their patterns of manipulation and victimhood, Frank had built a successful business, lived independently in San Francisco, and seemed to have figured out what was wrong with the family system.

The rest of the family's reaction to Frank was telling. Grandmother, my aunt, and my parents all warned me to stay away from him. He was "weird," they said, though they never specified exactly how. Looking back, Frank's weirdness was that he'd broken free from their dysfunction and refused to take part in their victim narratives.

Frank could articulate exactly what was wrong with our family. He understood that grandmother was the source of much of the toxicity, that the attacks on Grandfather were unconscionable, and that the entire system kept people trapped and dependent. He'd tried to help various family members with business opportunities, offering startup money and guidance, only to watch them sabotage themselves out of fear.

The family's warnings to avoid Frank weren't about protecting me–they were about protecting their worldview. Frank represented living proof that their limitations weren't universal truths, that someone could leave this dysfunction behind and be genuinely happy.

Over the years, Frank and I had several conversations that became lifelines for me. I was confused by the family dynamics, unable to articulate the toxicity or understand their motivations. Frank became my sounding board, willing to discuss the manipulation openly and help me navigate through the confusion.

He told me about his business ventures, his dreams and hopes, and the struggles he faced trying to maintain relationships with family members who seemed determined to undermine anyone who achieved independence. He clearly saw the patterns I was wrestling with and helped me understand that my confusion was a normal response to an abnormal situation.

I didn't see any signs of toxicity from Frank himself. He seemed honest but bewildered–a person who'd escaped the family system but was still processing the damage it had caused.

When Frank passed away from encephalitis, Pam called to tell me about the funeral. I couldn't attend, but I learned something that revealed the depths of her callousness. Frank had been cremated and had expressed wishes about being scattered at sea.

This is where Pam showed exactly who she was.

She simply put Frank's ashes in an urn, placed him on a shelf, and later moved him to the garage where she forgot about him. When you make a promise to a dying person, you keep it. That's sacred. That's basic human decency. But she couldn't be bothered to honor his simple last request.

I was stunned by her utter disrespect of her brother. Here was a man who had spent years trying to help family members, who had offered me guidance and understanding when I was struggling to make sense of the surrounding dysfunction. He'd been the only person in the family who told the truth about what was happening. And she treated his last wishes as if they didn't matter.

Frank's ashes sat in her garage for years because she forgot about him. As far as I know, they remain there to this day.

Any respect I might have had for her, and it wasn't much, disappeared completely when I learned this. Her utter disrespect for her brother boggled my mind. This wasn't just callousness–this was a fundamental lack of understanding about what it means to honor the dead, to keep your word, to show basic human respect.

The Long-Distance Victim

The family's toxic reach extended far beyond California. Joe, grandfather's brother living in New Jersey, discovered that 3,000 miles of distance couldn't protect him from systematic dysfunction.

Joe had served with distinction in World War II–his unit was among the first to break through the Siegfried Line into

Germany, earning a Presidential Citation. He'd built a successful life in real estate and investments, maintained a solid 32-year marriage, and seemed to have escaped the family's gravitational pull.

When I contacted Joe for family history information, he was initially cooperative but warned me:

"Some things I tell you may shock you!! As I was per-judged by individuals out there. That their minds were poisoned by listening to hearsay."

He'd experienced the family's characteristic approach to relationship management–condemning people based on manufactured narratives rather than direct experience.

The financial exploitation was telling. Joe had loaned Uncle Frank money, only to have Frank develop convenient "amnesia" about repayment.

"I got the money back, but I had to threaten him," Joe explained. "He only writes to you when he wants something. Same way as Pam."

Even Aunt Pam, despite living on the other coast, had written to Joe "numerous times" with "her hand out. Gimme, gimme, gimme."

Most revealing was what happened during Joe's major health crisis. When he had a heart attack and underwent angioplasty, his wife called Frank to inform the family. Frank never called the hospital or sent a card–not for two years afterward.

"Now, how would you feel if you was on the other side of that coin?" Joe asked me.

The same family that would later create elaborate memorial websites and perform grief publicly couldn't manage basic human decency during an actual medical emergency.

Joe's visit to California for his mother's funeral in 1973 perfectly captured the family's priorities. While grieving his mother's death, Grandmother complained that making the trip meant they "could have bought a refrigerator" instead. When Joe paid for the hotel, funeral expenses, and everything else, and then later sent them the plane fare money back, it still wasn't enough to earn basic respect or consideration.

Joe had to seek counseling from a VA therapist because the family's rejection "hurt me like hell." Here was a man who'd survived combat in World War II, built a successful business, and maintained healthy relationships–yet this family's cruelty could still inflict serious wounds.

Christmas Dinner

The Christmas dinner scene when I was 16 perfectly captured the toxic dynamics that defined our extended family gatherings. During what passed for conversation, my father casually announced, "I found your mom working on the street." My mother turned red and looked away. Whether true or not, it was a calculated act of cruelty designed to humiliate her in front of everyone.

But notice what happened next. Grandmother immediately started whining about how embarrassing this was for her, how she couldn't show her face in the neighborhood, how hard her life had become. Pam, meanwhile, made sympathetic noises while shooting meaningful looks around the table that said, "See what we have to deal with? Poor us, stuck with these people."

This was the environment I was expected to navigate under the rigid rule of "children should be seen and not heard." I learned that family members would use the most intimate knowledge they possessed as weapons against each other. I watched as cruel revelations became entertainment and saw how different family members responded to the same cruelty in ways that revealed their character.

The lesson was clear: proximity to family didn't guarantee safety or support. In fact, it often meant the opposite. The people who knew you best were the ones most capable of inflicting precise emotional damage.

I found refuge in books, even in grandmother's questionable collection of UFO and astrology materials. Reading became both escape and self-education. I was learning to be intellectually curious without depending on family for emotional support or validation.

The contrast between grandfather's dignified endurance and everyone else's tendency toward a victim mentality and cruelty shaped my understanding of how to handle suffering. He showed me it was possible to carry tremendous pain without becoming bitter or lashing out at others. The rest of them showed me what not to become.

The Steambath Escape

One Christmas visit when I was about sixteen, I sat in grandmother's living room and slowly died of boredom. The adults were clustered around the dining table, rehashing the same complaints and grievances they'd been nursing for decades. Children were supposed to be seen and not heard–something I'd heard from Dad repeatedly–so I was relegated to the corner with nothing but the television for company.

That's when "Steambath" came on. I think it was a play translated to a movie, starring Bill Bixby. Some philosophical thing about people trapped in what looks like a steambath but turns out to be purgatory. It was quite sophisticated–questions about death, judgment, the meaning of life.

I was glued to that TV for the entire show, finally finding something intellectually stimulating in this desert of forced family togetherness.

"Richard," Mom's voice cut through the television dialogue. "Come join the family discussion."

I waved her away without taking my eyes off the screen. "I'm watching something."

"Don't be rude to your mother," Dad's voice, sharper now. "Get over here."

"In a minute," I said, still focused on the TV. This was the most interesting thing that had happened in hours of mind-numbing family obligation.

"Richard!" Mom again, more insistent.

I waved them away again, more emphatically this time. For once, I'd found something worth paying attention to, something that engaged my brain instead of demanding I sit quietly while adults performed the same dysfunctional patterns they'd been rehearsing my entire life.

Dad's voice carried a warning edge. "You better get over here right now."

But I stayed put, absorbed in this weird little philosophical movie that was asking real questions about existence while my family recycled the same petty dramas. It was something interesting in a time when I was being forcibly introverted, when any display of curiosity or engagement was treated as disruption.

I finished watching the show, and years later I hunted it down again. It really was a nice little play. It represented something precious: proof that there were ideas worth exploring beyond the suffocating atmosphere of "children should be seen and not heard."

The fact that my parents tried to drag me away from the one intellectually stimulating thing in hours of family obligation perfectly captured the dynamic—they wanted my physical presence for their performance of family unity, but they had no interest in my actual engagement or curiosity about anything meaningful.

Grandfather eventually died from Alzheimer's — a final cruelty that slowly erased the precise memories he'd carried with such discipline for decades. Even in his decline, he maintained more dignity than the people who had spent years trying to tear him down.

Chapter 4: Family Life

Mom the Entrepreneur

It was strange to watch my parents navigate their way through creating a business. I think Mom would have preferred that Dad had remained employed at Norton or some other place. She was extremely uncomfortable, and that was the subject of many violent arguments, with basing their survival on income from dad's art.

Dad was tired of working for someone else because "there was so much corruption." He preferred the freedom of being an artist and self-employed rather than the prison of the workplace.

Mom's business adventures began with selling Tupperware and Avon. I remember boxes filled with glass bottles containing weird scents, catalogs, and piles of plastic sealable containers. Mom used to drag me around to Tupperware and Avon parties, and I tried to stay small in the corner while my mom morphed into a salesperson and the ladies enjoyed smelling scents and examining the plastic containers.

I knew to remain hidden and be quiet. Mom was busy. During these sales events, she could become ruthless if I acted up or didn't follow her direction. I essentially became her servant, carrying in the boxes and returning them to the car.

"This one's perfect for salads," Mom would say, lifting an empty container like she was presenting the crown jewels. "See how the seal keeps everything fresh?"

The women nodded and murmured appreciation, their fingers testing the snap of lids, the satisfaction of a perfect seal.

Then she'd become an Avon lady, selling cosmetics and perfumes. I was fascinated by all the different bottle shapes and sizes–they looked like tiny works of art. The house would fill with competing fragrances during her parties, floral perfumes mixing with fruity body sprays and musky colognes until the air was almost thick enough to taste.

She also ran a local Brownie troop, basically Girl Scouts for younger kids. Once again, no babysitter budget, so I got stuffed into corners with books while surrounded by girl activities that I completely ignored.

There was always a certain amount of desperation in Mom's entrepreneurship. She took it seriously and was always looking for a new way to bring in money. It was as if her life depended on it.

The Artist's Evolution

Dad's artistic journey had started differently. His talent had emerged early, but in an environment that saw creativity as a weakness. As he told an interviewer years later: "Artists in my family were frowned upon. They were kind of like fairies and queers, that didn't really work hard to make a living… you know, the reputation that artists always have."

This early dismissal had forced him to approach his talent strategically rather than romantically. In the military, he'd painted portraits of generals and colonels, trading artistic skill for career advancement. He understood that creativity had to prove its worth in terms other people valued–recognition, money, influence.

"I really didn't do anything until after I went into the service. I decided I had this talent, and I started painting portraits of generals and colonels and whatever. And they discovered they could put me to good use. And that's how I got to do all these portraits of these V.I.P.'s and stuff. That's how I got my excellent reputation in the service."

His military record told the story of professional advancement through artistic competence. Commendation after commendation praised not just his technical skill but his ability to work independently and meet impossible deadlines. He'd painted portraits of Presidents Kennedy, Johnson, Eisenhower, and Nixon not because he was passionate about political figures, but because those commissions opened doors and established credentials.

But the family's early dismissal of his artistic aspirations had lasting effects. He never seemed to fully trust that his creative work had intrinsic value. When asked about all his military commendations, he said bitterly: "Yeah, and with all those and 35¢ I could have bought a can of beer. But they make you feel wanted… what I wanted they couldn't give me."

What he wanted was promotion to officer rank, recognition that his contributions mattered beyond just being useful. "I wanted a promotion to an officer. As you can see there, I was recommended many times for a commission, but I always turned it down like a damn fool." The joy of creation was always shadowed by the need to prove that art wasn't just self-indulgent fantasy.

Dad's Contradictions

In his makeshift art studio, Dad transformed into someone I barely recognized. His pen-and-ink drawings covered our living room walls–generals, admirals, presidents, every military rank rendered in meticulous detail. Each portrait captured not just the face but the character, the weight of command, the burden of authority.

"Look at this one," he'd say, holding up a group portrait with forty individual faces surrounding General MacArthur. "Each person took me three hours. Had to get the insignia exactly right."

His hands moved across the paper like a surgeon's, every line deliberate, every shadow calculated. The same intensity that exploded in rage could create remarkable beauty when properly channeled.

The oil paintings differed from the pen-and-ink work. Thicker, more emotional, built up in layers you could feel with your fingertips. The Churchill portrait dominated one wall, masterfully executed except for the extra finger on the left hand. Even artistic skill had its mistakes.

The garage studio was thick with turpentine and linseed oil, chemical smells that made my eyes water and my head swim. But I loved running my hands over the finished pieces, feeling mountains that had actual ridges, faces with raised cheekbones, uniforms with buttons that cast actual shadows.

Dad's garden transformed our backyard into something from a nature documentary. Flower beds arranged in geometric patterns, each one carefully planned and executed with the same precision he brought to his artwork. The air buzzed with bees and butterflies, thick with the scent of marigolds and roses.

I could lose entire afternoons out there, watching insects move through their routines. My collection of specimens grew–beetles pinned to cork boards, butterflies preserved in resin, each one labeled with scientific accuracy that would have impressed a graduate student.

Time disappeared when I was cataloging. Six hours felt like twenty minutes. The world beyond the garden fence ceased to exist.

Best of all, the garden was a place where I could hide from the continual arguments between my parents. I knew every path, ridge, anthill, and wasp nest in the backyard. Although it was my dad's garden, it was my domain.

These moments of beauty and creation were real. Dad's artistic talent was genuine, his attention to detail remarkable, his ability to capture both technical accuracy and emotional depth in his work undeniable. But none of this changed the fact that he could look at his own child and declare ownership like I was farm equipment.

But Dad's contradictions extended beyond art. The magazines that filled our coffee table–Better Homes and Gardens, Good Housekeeping, Family Circle–became my inadvertent education in adult aspiration. I'd cut out pictures of women from the advertisements, fascinated by their smiles and perfect hair, the way they looked so confident and happy.

Dad caught me with my pile of cutout women one afternoon, his eyebrows rising with that expression that meant I'd done something worth mocking.

"Having fantasies about pretty ladies?" he said, his voice dripping with sarcasm. "You're dreaming if you think women like that would ever love someone like you."

The message was clear: beauty was for other people, love was for other people, and I shouldn't aim above my station.

When I discovered Playboy at the magazine stand, Dad caught me looking and made an offer that sounded too good to be true.

"If you ever want a subscription to that, just let me know," he said with a wink. "I'll get it for you."

Six months later, I took him up on it.

"I never said that," he replied when I brought it up. "It would never embarrass your mother. I won't expose her to that kind of garbage."

"But you did say it. I remember exactly."

"I never would have said such a thing."

"Would you prefer I sneak around and look at it behind your back?"

He paused, considering the options. "Yes."

Another lesson in the family's mechanics: offers would be denied, promises would be broken, and honesty would be punished while deception was quietly endorsed.

I vividly remember when Deep Throat became a big hit. My parents went to see it, came home all lovey-dovey, and quickly headed to the bedroom. Lots of noise. Even as a kid, I understood the connection between what they'd seen and their behavior afterward.

Art calmed him like nothing else could. When he was painting, the house filled with blessed silence instead of shouting. But the contradictions in his character–the same hands that created beauty could destroy innocence without explanation–were teaching me that people contained multitudes, most of them dangerous.

I remember watching Dad paint and draw. He became immersed in the craft with all his attention on making all the details perfect.

Best of all, when he was painting or drawing, he left me alone. He gave no incrimination or demand. He simply painted. Mom left him alone at these times, so there were no arguments.

Funny how later in life, his hyperfocus on something creative became my standard for relaxation and escape.

Their Love Story

My parents' love story began with genuine romance. When Dad shipped out to Alaska in 1957, just days after their wedding, Mom wrote him letters that revealed a depth of feeling I never saw between them during my childhood:

"Oh, my darling I miss you so terribly that I don't know how I am going to stand being away from you… Last night when I saw you leaving on that bus & you were waving goodbye, I almost stopped the bus. It broke my heart to see you ride out of my life for these next horrible months."

That letter, written in 1957, captured something the raw emotional connection without the defensive barriers that would later define their relationship. My mother was 18 years old, writing with the vulnerability of someone who hadn't yet learned to weaponize her so-called pain.

But even then, the seeds of future conflict were visible. In that same letter, she railed against the Air Force system that separated enlisted men from their wives while allowing officers to bring their families: "Doesn't the service have a heart or is it strictly military not caring about if the wives are with the lower rank men… Are they supposed to be better than the ordinary man?"

The class resentment, the sense of being treated unfairly by those with more power, the righteous anger at systematic injustice–all the themes that would later poison family gatherings were already present. My mother had identified a real inequity, but instead of channeling that observation into constructive action, she made it part of her identity as someone the world treated unfairly.

Unfortunately, that type of love didn't last long. My mom seemed to feel that life had dealt her a terrible card. She seemed to be filled with a simmering disgust that later evolved into covert maliciousness.

Their love evolved into a classic co-dependency that dominated their lives.

Unfortunately, I didn't realize this pattern until much later in life. My own relationships suffered from the same issues until I realized what was happening and put a stop to it.

When Success Made Everything Worse

By the time I reached my teens, the business pressure had transformed our household into something even more toxic. The kitchen became a battlefield every morning, the air thick with resentment and the smell of burnt coffee.

Mom stood at the sink, shoulders rigid with tension, while Dad sat at the table reading his newspaper like a shield against conversation.

"We're behind on the mortgage again," Mom would say, her voice carrying the weight of sleepless nights and impossible calculations.

"I'm working as much as I can," Dad would reply without looking up.

"But it's not enough. It's never enough."

"Then what do you want me to do? Rob a bank?"

The arguments followed the same script every day, with minor variations in volume and viciousness. Money, sex, money, sex, round and round like a broken record that someone kept flipping over to play again.

I learned to eat breakfast quickly and disappear before the real shouting started.

But I was also watching how Dad handled Mom's depression, which seemed to cycle like the phases of the moon. When the darkness hit her, when she'd spend days in bed barely speaking, Dad would appear with packages. New furniture for the living room, clothes she'd never wear, antiques that would sit gathering dust. The purchases came charged to revolving credit lines that multiplied through our financial system.

"Look what I got you, honey," he'd say, unwrapping whatever treasure he'd bought that day. "Thought you'd like this."

Mom's face would brighten temporarily, like sunlight breaking through storm clouds. The depression would lift for a few days, maybe a week, then settle back over her like fog rolling in from the ocean. Dad would reach for his wallet again. To make Mom happy, he sold their bonds, took out lines of credit, and dipped into savings.

The financial pressure of their art business was making Dad even more controlling and violent. After Dad's vasectomy, something fundamental shifted in his personality. The procedure took place on a Tuesday, and he came home that evening walking carefully, wincing with each step. But the physical pain healed faster than whatever had broken inside his head.

He became sullen, distant, checking out as a parent in ways that made his previous emotional distance seem warm by comparison. The phrases "You're my child" and "You'll do what I tell you" became more frequent, delivered with an edge that made it clear he saw me as property rather than a person.

When I was ten, Dad needed his gallbladder removed. The night before he went to the hospital, he called me into the living room, his face serious in *that way* that meant something important was about to happen.

"Richard, while I'm gone, you're going to be the man of the house," he said, looking at me with those intense eyes that seemed to catalog everything around him.

I stared back at him completely bewildered. "What does that mean?"

"Just… be the man of the house. You'll figure it out."

That was it. No explanation, no guidance, no clarification of what responsibilities came with this mysterious title. I was ten years old, still collecting comic books and building model airplanes, and suddenly I was supposed to understand some adult concept he couldn't be bothered to explain.

As all these experiences accumulated, I withdrew even more. The constant warfare between my parents wore me down. I didn't want anything to do with anyone except my small crew of friends–three or four of us who played elaborate war games with model kits, rode bikes like maniacs, hung around at school, and stayed off the adult radar.

You Did It

I was in the living room, watching Gilligan's Island on our black and white television. Our cat sat beside me, purring while I scratched her head.

Dad appeared in the room, looking haggard. He sat across from me in a chair, turned off the television, and said he had something important to say.

"Mom just tried to kill herself." He said this matter-of-factly, like it was an everyday occurrence. His shirt was soaked with water as if he'd taken a shower in his clothes. There was an unfathomable look on his face. I couldn't decide whether he was angry or sad or something else.

I just looked at him; the words meant nothing to me.

"I said, your mom just tried to kill herself."

"Umm."

"Don't you care?"

Thoughts were rattling around in my head. Life without Mom? Would that mean the fights would stop? Or would Dad become even more vicious and mean?

Dad stared at me for a long moment. "You know why she wanted to kill herself?"

"No." Why would I have any idea about that?

"Because of you."

"Me?" I struggled to keep the tears from flowing to my face. Why would my mom want to take her own life because of me? But I didn't cry because I knew that Dad's belt was always ready.

"You. You won't shut up. You make noise all the time. You chatter. You ask questions. You drive her crazy. Won't you just shut up?"

I didn't know what to say.

He didn't give me a chance to answer. "Why can't you just be quiet? Do something productive. You know, you're never going to be anything. You're just a little brat, spoiled, always asking for things. You don't want to work. You don't support us. Do you understand that I own you?"

I felt something fundamental break inside my understanding of how families worked. Not only was I responsible for being quiet and obedient and invisible, I was literally responsible for keeping my mother alive through the sheer act of not being myself.

The silence that followed differed from any quiet I'd experienced before. It was heavy, full of things that couldn't be unsaid. I wanted to ask if Mom was okay, if she was still in the bathroom, if there was blood like when my sister stepped on glass. But asking questions had apparently driven her to this, so asking more questions seemed dangerous.

"Is she…" I started, then stopped.

"She's alive," Dad said. "But things are going to be different now. You understand me?"

I nodded, though I didn't understand anything except that my natural personality, my curiosity, my need for interaction… all of it was toxic. Deadly, even. The solution was to become smaller, quieter, more invisible than ever before.

I ran to my room and cried for the rest of the day.

My ears began picking up conversations through walls, whispered arguments in their bedroom, phone calls that stopped when I walked into a room. The skill developed out of necessity–information meant survival, and I needed to know which direction trouble was coming from, especially now that I apparently had the power to kill people just by being myself.

The Gallery Dream

Dad began painting animals in watercolor. He enjoyed that much more than the black and white portraits he drew for the officers at Norton. I always thought his portraits were incredible. His watercolor wildlife art was good, but a little too technical for me. Every hair on every feather was perfect.

They both soon realized that they had an opportunity to sell his art, and we began attending art shows all over the local area. These are small shows put on by local businesses. The art was displayed on homemade A-frames in rows, so that customers could view them and select their purchases.

After a few years, these weekend art show successes convinced them to take the ultimate risk. Dad quit his civil service job to focus on art full time while Mom handled business development. They moved to Lake Arrowhead and opened their own gallery, transforming Dad's artistic talent and Mom's business skills into a sustainable enterprise.

"My top salary was just under twelve thousand dollars a year. The civil service didn't treat you too well. Mostly dead-beats and dead-heads worked in civil service. And that's the reason I never got along with them… because I like to work hard and perform my functions and get my job done."

The gallery became a showcase for Dad's evolution as an artist. His pen-and-ink military portraits gave way to watercolor wildlife paintings that combined technical precision with genuine artistic vision. By the time he was featured in regional art magazines, critics were comparing his work to Audubon and calling him "the world's most technically precise wildlife painter."

"I love it. Do you? I sure do. The only thing that bothers me is the way mother feels about it."

"How does mom feel about it?"

"A steady check coming in every week is the best thing in the world. I don't particularly care for that, because I know I can make more."

Their success was accidental–the two had no business acumen or training. Dad studied animal anatomy with the same precision he'd once applied to military technical illustrations.

The problem was simple. Because they lacked a business plan and skill, any successes resulted from chance.

That translated to a feast or famine environment. One month they'd make more than enough money, the next almost nothing.

This hampered me throughout my adult life. It took me decades to realize that feast or famine is not a healthy or desirable way to run a business.

Chapter 5: Institution Failures

When the Good Shepherd Showed His True Nature

Dad was deeply devout, at least on Sundays. His church attendance was perfect; his prayers were elaborate performances of piety. And don't let me forget the prayers before dinner, with hands linked, and evening prayer before going to bed.

Every week we'd sit in those wooden pews that made my legs go numb, listening to hymns that bored me senselessly and sermons designed to make people feel guilty about being human.

"Be still," Dad would whisper if I so much as shifted position. "Don't embarrass me."

If I moved too much or made any noise, he'd grab my arm and drag me out behind the church for a beating calculated to hurt without leaving marks. Then we'd return to our pew, him smiling and nodding at fellow parishioners like nothing had happened.

I learned to sit motionless for hours, unfocusing my eyes, my mind racing through books I'd read, projects I wanted to build, anything that could distract me from the aching boredom and my total lack of understanding as to what they were talking about. The same focus that let me read for eight hours straight became a survival tool for enduring religious theater.

The Church of Christ took pride in doing everything "by the book" - meaning exactly as written in the Bible, with no additions or interpretations. No musical instruments during worship because the Bible didn't specifically mention them. No church hierarchy beyond local elders because that's how the church operated. Every doctrine had to be backed up with chapter and verse citations.

This made the hypocrisy even more jarring when it appeared. These people spent hours debating whether communion bread should be leavened or unleavened based on scriptural accuracy but somehow missed the obvious commandments about protecting children. The same precision that governed every ritual detail disappeared completely for actual moral behavior.

This was the Church of Christ, and piety, humbleness, and servitude were the order of every Sunday.

When I was ten, I saw something that shattered the whole facade.

I caught the minister with a young girl, maybe twelve years old, doing things that made my stomach clench with horror. The details don't matter. What mattered was that it was wrong–clearly, obviously wrong–happening in the place that was supposed to be safest. This was supposedly the house of God!

Everything I'd been taught about goodness and authority collapsed in that moment. If the man who preached about morality every Sunday was capable of this, then what did any of it mean? The building, the rituals, the prayers–maybe it was all just performance.

I sat in the back seat while my father drove home, my mind numb. I kept trying to make sense of what I'd seen. This was the man who talked about protecting innocence, about God's love for children. This was the person my father held up as an example of Christian virtue.

I told Dad immediately. A child was being hurt. Adults were supposed to protect children when that happened.

"You're lying," he said flatly. "You must have seen something else. Misunderstood what was happening."

"I saw what I saw. He was hurting her."

Dad's face hardened. "You're wrong. And if I hear you spreading lies about good Christian people, you'll be in serious trouble."

Standing there in our living room, watching my father choose the reputation of an abuser over the safety of a child, I understood something fundamental. Adults didn't protect children when it was inconvenient. Institutions didn't serve justice when it threatened their image. The moral framework I'd been taught was optional, applied only when convenient.

But I was also learning something else: my eyes worked fine, even when adults wanted to pretend they didn't.

The same pattern showed up everywhere I looked.

When Evidence Doesn't Matter

Law enforcement seemed to operate under the same rules. My sister's bike accident happened right in front of our house, and I watched the whole thing from our front yard. She'd stopped at the roadside exactly like our parents had taught us, waiting for the car to pass before crossing.

Instead, the driver swerved directly into her.

There was no ambiguity. The car deliberately changed course to hit my sister, smashing her bike and sending her rolling across the pavement. I saw every detail–the trajectory change, the deliberate steering change, the driver's face through the windshield.

When the police arrived, they immediately decided the driver wasn't at fault.

"But I saw what happened," I told the investigating officer. "The car swerved into her."

He barely glanced at me. "Kids don't always see things clearly. Your sister probably moved into the road without looking."

"No, she didn't! She was stopped exactly where she was supposed to be!"

"Son," the officer said in that condescending tone adults used when they'd already made up their minds, "accidents happen. Your sister's fine, that's what matters."

Standing there arguing with him while my sister's bike lay twisted in the street, I realized something important. My observations didn't matter to adults who'd already decided what they wanted to believe. Truth was less important than convenience.

School wasn't any different.

School: Where Different Meant Wrong

The educational system revealed the same pattern, just more subtly. Teachers talked constantly about helping every child reach their potential, but their actions showed they meant helping every child fit the same mold.

Fourth grade brought square dancing. Mrs. Peterson announced it with forced enthusiasm: "We're going to learn square dancing!"

The pairing process was social execution disguised as education. Girls picked boys one by one until everyone was matched. I stood against the wall, watching my classmates pair off, my stomach sinking with each selection that wasn't me.

I was the last one chosen. Of course.

"Ha! Richard gets to dance with the ugliest girl in school because he's the ugliest boy!" someone shouted from across the room.

The teacher heard it. She saw my face flush with humiliation. But instead of addressing the cruelty or questioning a system that guaranteed public shame for some students, she just smiled and told us to get into position.

That moment created a permanent aversion that lasted decades. I never danced again–not at weddings, not at parties, nowhere. The school had taught me that taking part in social activities meant risking public degradation, and they were fine with that outcome.

My grades crashed in fifth grade. The subjects felt pointless, the homework impossible, the entire system designed for brains that worked nothing like mine. I could focus on insects for six hours straight but couldn't concentrate on math worksheets for five minutes.

When I tried to explain how my mind worked differently, the response was always the same: try harder, pay attention, apply yourself. The possibility that their methods might not work for everyone never entered the conversation.

School taught me that institutions valued conformity over curiosity, obedience over intelligence, sitting still over thinking creatively. Students who didn't fit the standard model were treated as defective rather than different.

Building My Own Standards

By age twelve, I'd figured out some things that a lot of adults seemed to have missed.

Adults lied when it was easier than dealing with problems. They'd choose what they wanted to believe over what happened, especially if the truth made their lives more complicated. My eyes worked fine, but that didn't matter if what I saw made adults uncomfortable.

The rules changed depending on who was involved. Ministers could hurt kids but still be "good Christian people." Drivers could hit cyclists, but it was somehow the cyclist's fault. Teachers could let kids get humiliated in front of everyone if it served their lesson plan.

I couldn't count on grown-ups to make sense or be fair. They had their own reasons for doing things, and those reasons usually had nothing to do with what they said they cared about.

So, I started paying attention to what people did instead of what they said they were doing. I looked for the patterns that showed what they really cared about. And I stopped expecting the official version of anything to match what I could see with my own eyes.

I just knew I needed to figure things out for myself, because the people who were supposed to have answers either didn't know or didn't care enough to tell the truth.

Chapter 6: Childhood Friends and Fears

The Last Good Years

During my early elementary years at Cypress and Hillside, I was the kid who made friends easily. Gregarious, happy, the type who'd walk up to anyone and start a conversation. That would change, but in those early years, the retreat hadn't started yet.

At our first place in Rialto, I had three friends: Paul, Kenny, and Tommy. Behind the apartment complex stretched a dry field where we could build forts, dig trenches, and stage elaborate battles, sometimes throwing dirt clods at each other.

But our real treasure was another field, hidden from our house by a wall of grass and fallen tree branches. Our secret territory, where adults couldn't see us.

"Let's build a fort," Paul would announce, and we'd spend hours constructing defensive positions with sticks and dirt.

"Mine's bigger," Kenny would counter, piling rocks higher around his bunker.

"Size doesn't matter if you can't defend it," Tommy would say, already planning his attack strategy.

We'd fight epic battles with water pistols, absorbed in our war games. The rest of the world disappeared during those sessions. No arguing parents, no household tension, just four kids lost in elaborate fantasy scenarios.

One afternoon, we were building a particularly ambitious fort when a young man emerged from the trees. Maybe 24 or 25, slightly disheveled but smiling in a way that seemed harmless enough.

"Hey guys," he said, settling cross-legged near our construction project. "What are you building?"

"A fort," I said proudly, gesturing at our pile of sticks and stones.

"Cool. You know what would be even better? A teepee. I could show you how to build a real one with these branches."

I didn't know what a teepee was, but it sounded fascinating. "Sure!"

We spent the entire day working under his guidance, learning to lash branches together, creating a structure tall enough for all of us to sit inside comfortably. As the sun started setting, we crawled inside our masterpiece.

"Now," the young man said, pulling out a flashlight, "every teepee needs ghost stories."

He held the flashlight under his chin, casting eerie shadows across his face. "There once was an Indian brave who got lost in these very woods…"

We were completely captivated, huddled together in our makeshift shelter as his voice rose and fell with the story. The flashlight beam danced across the woven branches above us, creating moving shadows that made the tale come alive.

Then the wall of branches exploded inward.

"WHAT THE HELL IS GOING ON HERE?"

My father stood in the ruins of our teepee, his face contorted with rage and what I now recognize was genuine terror. The young man scrambled backward, the flashlight flying from his hands.

"I was just… we were building…" the man stammered.

"GET AWAY FROM THESE KIDS!" Dad roared. "GET OUT OF HERE BEFORE I CALL THE POLICE!"

The young man ran, crashing through the underbrush like a spooked deer. Dad grabbed me by the arm and dragged me toward home while Paul, Kenny, and Tommy scattered in different directions.

"Don't you ever talk to strangers again," Dad said, his grip tight enough to leave marks. His voice was shaking - not with anger this time, but with fear. "Do you understand me? EVER. Men like that take children. They hurt them. They make them disappear."

I nodded, confused and scared. The man had seemed nice. We'd had fun building the teepee. But Dad's reaction told me I'd walked into danger I couldn't see, that I'd been seconds away from something terrible happening.

Looking back now, I understand Dad's terror. A strange adult male luring four young boys into an enclosed space as darkness fell—every parent's nightmare. But at the time, it felt like another adult destroying something good for reasons that made no sense.

At least this time, he didn't take out the belt. His fear had overwhelmed his anger.

After the Move

After that, we moved to the house in Rialto, the one with the footlocker that contained grandees and military hardware. We didn't stay there long, and I don't remember making any friends. My primary companion was my sister, and I was keeping a closer eye on her since her epileptic attack.

When we finally settled on Stoddard Avenue, closer to the San Gabriel Mountains, I was in second grade. The family chaos was escalating, but I was still trying to maintain normal friendships.

But something was changing in me. The calm confidence that had made friends come naturally was cracking. I watched other kids more carefully, trying to figure out if they were safe to trust.

The arguments at home were getting louder and more frequent, and I was becoming more aware of how different our family was from others. I still made friends, but it required more effort now, more calculation. The part of me that used to just walk up to anyone and start talking was learning to be cautious first.

David: A Window Into Normal

David became my best friend. He lived across the street with his mother, and they were both Jewish, the only Jewish people I knew as a child. Usually, he came over to my house, but the few times I visited his place opened my eyes to how different families could be.

"Come look at this," David said one afternoon, leading me to a display case with glass fronts and sides.

The case was filled with artifacts I'd never seen before. Silver cups, ornate books, strange implements that looked both ancient and valuable. Everything was carefully arranged, obviously treasured.

"What are they?" I asked, pressing my nose against the glass.

"Religious stuff," David said casually. "My mom says they're from my great-grandfather in Europe."

I stared at the collection, mesmerized. In our house, valuable things got broken during arguments or "accidentally" destroyed when someone was angry. Here, precious objects were protected, displayed, treated with obvious respect.

"When I grow up," I announced, "I'm going to have display cases like this."

David laughed. "For what?"

"Rocks. Models. Important stuff."

I meant it. The sight of those carefully preserved treasures made something click inside me. Valuable things deserve protection. Important collections needed proper homes.

Years later, I would indeed have three display cases, one for my rock collection, one for knives, one for painted miniatures. But that day in David's living room was the first time I understood collections could be more than just accumulated objects. They could be statements about what you valued, what you thought worth preserving.

Chris: Recognizing Worse

Another friend was Chris, slightly younger than David and me. He hung around us constantly, and I think he saw us as big brothers or mentors. His mom, Nancy, was tough as nails, the kind of woman who built patios and broke up concrete with hand tools. But Chris's father Kurt was a different kind of dangerous than my dad.

I saw Kurt hit Chris with a pipe and with his fists. Physical violence that made my father's calculated cruelty look almost restrained by comparison.

"Does it hurt?" I asked Chris one afternoon, noticing fresh bruises on his arms.

Chris shrugged. "He gets mad sometimes. It's not that bad."

But I could see it was that bad. Chris was developing the same watchfulness I recognized in myself, the same careful attention to adult moods and warning signs. The difference was that his father's explosions were immediate and physical, while mine were mental and often delayed.

One day Chris dragged me upstairs to his room, his eyes bright with mischief.

"Want to see something cool?" he whispered.

My stomach was clenched. "What kind of something?"

"Dad's got magazines under his bed. Want to look?"

Every instinct screamed danger, but curiosity won. We crept into his dad's bedroom, and Chris pulled out stacks of men's magazines. Compared to what's available now, they were tame, mostly topless shots with everything else airbrushed. But back then, they seemed incredibly racy.

We giggled and whispered comments, then carefully replaced everything exactly where we'd found it. But walking home, I felt the same sick sensation I'd experienced finding Dad's metal box in the closet. That sense of stumbling into adult territory where children weren't supposed to be, of seeing things that would somehow change me in ways I couldn't understand yet.

I never went back to that bedroom. Something about the entire experience felt contaminated, connected to secrets that adults kept from children for reasons that were probably good.

When Systems Failed

My dad tried to enroll me in Webelos, the Boy Scout program for younger kids. The meeting was held in someone's garage with about forty kids sitting in rows while a couple of adult leaders explained the program with forced enthusiasm.

"We're going to learn outdoor skills," one leader announced. "Camping, hiking, working together as a team."

The other kids seemed excited, but the sheer number of people in that enclosed space made my chest tight. Forty kids plus adults, all talking and moving at once, following instructions shouted over the noise. The artificial cheerfulness, the way the adults tried to organize our activities according to some manual rather than letting things develop naturally.

This felt exactly like the church, the school classroom, every other place where adults herded large groups of children and expected us all to respond the same way. The same instinct that made me distrust other institutional authority was picking up familiar warning signals.

Halfway through the meeting, I started crying. Not just sniffling - full-blown, uncontrollable sobbing that I couldn't explain or stop. The noise, the crowd, the forced group activities - it all felt overwhelming in a way I couldn't put into words.

"What's wrong, son?" one leader asked, kneeling beside me while forty other kids turned to stare.

"I don't know," I hiccupped. "I want to go home."

They called my parents, and I never went back. I won a geology badge during that single meeting, but the entire experience felt wrong in ways I couldn't articulate. Looking back, I think it was the combination of too many people, artificial structure, and adults trying to manufacture childhood experiences according to predetermined patterns instead of letting kids figure things out naturally.

Large groups of children being managed by adults who followed scripts–that was a recipe for disaster as far as my brain was concerned.

The Good Father

One genuinely good thing my dad did during this period was take me rock hunting. During trips to art shows, we'd make stops to search for specimens. The desert was full of rock shops, and Dad seemed to genuinely enjoy helping me build my collection.

"Look at this," he said one afternoon in Palm Springs, kneeling beside an old volcanic formation. "See how the quartz crystals formed in the cavities?"

He handed me a clear crystal about the size of my thumb, its faceted surface catching the desert sunlight.

"Can I keep it?"

"Of course. That's why we're here."

These were some of the few times I saw Dad actually happy, other than when he was painting. He enjoyed being outdoors, away from the household tension, focused on something concrete and discoverable. He knew nothing about geology and minerals, but I'd read a few books.

I'd point out different formations, explain how geological processes worked, and share what I'd learned about geology from my reading.

"This one's an arrowhead," I said, showing him a piece of worked flint. "Indians used to hunt all through these areas."

These were magical moments. It was one of the few times in my entire relationship with my father that he actually listened to me with respect.

My rock collection grew steadily, most specimens coming from Dad in one form or another. He even brought home drilling cores he stole from his work at Norton, fascinating cross-sections that showed layers of earth formed over millions of years.

In junior high school, I threw my entire rock collection away. Everything except a few small pieces I'd hidden in a drawer and forgotten about.

Why? Because they were from Dad, and by then our house had become a war zone. Money was getting tight, which meant constant arguments about bills and jobs. Mom and

Dad's relationship had turned cold and frosty - they barely spoke to each other except to fight about practical matters. Dad was looking for work while trying to keep his art career going. Mom was talking about getting a job herself, something that seemed to terrify Dad.

The few good moments we'd shared rock hunting felt contaminated by everything else. The constant verbal abuse, the escalating household tension, the way Dad could switch from enjoying a geology discussion to calling me worthless within the same hour. Those crystals and specimens sitting on my shelf had become reminders of a relationship that was mostly poison with occasional moments of humanity mixed in.

I couldn't separate the good parts from the bad anymore. They'd all gotten tangled up together.

Standing over the garbage can, dropping specimen after specimen into the trash, I felt like I was performing surgery on my own life. Cutting away anything that connected me to him, even the few positive memories, because they'd become impossible to separate from all the damage.

It didn't work, of course. I still lived with them and would for several more years. But throwing away those rocks felt like taking control of something, even if it was just my own possessions. If I couldn't escape the chaos, at least I could choose what reminders to keep around.

Eighth Grade Birthday

The week before my birthday, the kitchen smelled of vanilla and lemon cleaner. Mom set out the party box: paper hats, a wrinkled banner, the blindfold for Pin the Tail on the Donkey, the Twister mat held with a tired rubber band.

"Saturday at two," she said, tapping her list. "Hot dogs, cake, games. It'll be nice."

"I don't want a party," I said.

Her smile faded slightly, then she kept going, ignoring what I said. "We'll keep it small."

"I don't want one," I said again. "No party."

Silence. The fridge hummed. The wall clock ticked like a drip. She didn't ask why. She never did. I was just a child, her child, and my role was to do what I was told.

Dad walked in on the middle of it, set his keys on the counter, and took in the scene. "What's going on?"

"He says he doesn't want a party," Mom said, voice catching.

Dad looked at me, then at the banner. His mouth flattened. "You're having one," he said. "That's that."

I felt the click of a door closing inside me. "Okay," I said, voice neutral. I knew not to go against my dad, lest the belt come out. I knew that belt too well.

Saturday smelled like hot dogs and frosting. By two o'clock, shoes thumped on the porch and the doorbell rang in little bursts. Kids I knew from school filled the living room in paper hats. Mom's smile was back, bright and busy. "Spin him around," someone said, and hands turned me under the blindfold until the room shifted under my feet.

"Pin the tail," Dad laughed from the doorway, folding his arms, satisfied the program was back on track.

We played Twister; the vinyl mat squeaked under socks. We sang over candles that sparked. I blew them out and tasted sugar and wax. The gifts were small and neat. I said thank you in the right places. The noise rose and fell in waves I let pass through me.

Mom moved like a conductor, cueing games, slicing cake, pressing napkins into sticky hands, glowing under the lights she'd strung across the window. Dad hovered at the edge, pleased with order restored.

Inside, I kept still. I had closed the door to feelings by then. I couldn't afford them. I smiled when it was expected. I posed for a photo with the banner taped behind me, the blindfold folded on the coffee table, the tail pinned roughly where it belonged.

When the last kid left and the door clicked shut, the house exhaled. Frosting smears on plates. A curl of ribbon on the rug. Mom stacked paper cups, humming. Dad nodded once, verdict delivered and carried out.

I took my slice of leftover cake to my room, set it on the desk, and stared at the model kits on my bookshelf. The party happened. It wasn't mine. I'd been forced, not for the first time, to do something that someone else wanted me to do. It didn't feel good.

Years later, I could name it. It wasn't about cake. Mom was selfish. I was a child; children mostly think about themselves.

Mom was an adult. Her responsibility was to ask why and listen. She got hurt (or as they put it today, butthurt) instead, on cue, like a trick that worked on my dad, and she figured it would work on me. It didn't. It pushed me farther away .

In that bright kitchen, lemon sharp in the air, her tears were the entire show. The list on the counter, the banner folded along old creases, the blindfold smoothed flat with her palm, props waiting for a part I was refusing to play. By then, I had shut the door on feelings. I couldn't afford them. I stood there and let the scene pass over me like weather, and when it was done, I carried the silence upstairs and learned how to keep it.

When Help Wasn't Available

School has changed. Earlier teachers understood and helped. They actively listened to their students, intervened when needed, and maintained order.

The teachers from the 5th grade onward were useless.

Mrs. Henderson saw my grades dropping but blamed it on not trying hard enough.

Mr. Phillips, the principal, was more interested in avoiding problems than solving them.

The few times adults noticed something was wrong, their response was always the same: work harder, pay attention, apply yourself.

"Richard seems distracted lately," I overheard Mrs. Henderson telling another teacher. "Maybe he needs more structure at home."

If only she knew. Structure wasn't the problem. Unpredictable violence and manipulation was the problem. But in those days, school counselors weren't available. Verbal and mental abuse simply wasn't acknowledged as real abuse. And I wouldn't have known to ask for help anyway, since this was the only family life I'd ever known. I had nothing to compare it with, except for Chris, and his situation was so bad that mine looked like paradise in comparison.

Maybe all families had some kind of fury directed at children. Maybe this was just how adults were.

Over time, I was beginning to see that the only person I could depend on was me.

Building Underground Networks

As the family chaos escalated, I was learning to build informal networks of information and safety. These weren't just friendships–they were survival systems disguised as play.

Joy lived three houses down, a woman in her thirties with blonde hair and a smile that seemed genuinely warm instead of the practiced variety I'd grown used to from adults. She was always friendly when she saw me, asking about school or my latest model project with what felt like real interest.

"How's that airplane coming along, Richard?" she'd ask, leaning over her fence while she worked in her garden.

"Almost finished," I'd say, wanting to continue the conversation instead of looking for escape routes.

Joy treated me as if I were worth talking to, like my thoughts and projects mattered. She'd listen to my explanations about model kits or comic books without the glazed expression most adults got when children talked about things they cared about.

But Joy was having an affair with someone in the neighborhood, and when the news broke, she became a pariah overnight. Neighbors who'd chatted with her over fences suddenly found urgent business elsewhere when she appeared. The women from Mom's Tupperware and Avon circles spoke about her in whispered tones that carried more venom than anything they'd directed at genuinely dangerous people.

"She's not the kind of person you should be talking to anymore," Mom told me when she caught me waving at Joy.

"Why not? She's always nice to me."

"She's made some terrible choices. People are going to judge her for that."

Watching Joy get exiled for adult complications I didn't understand taught me that social approval and actual character had no relationship with each other. The kindest adult in my neighborhood had become untouchable because of relationship drama, while genuinely harmful people continued to receive respect as long as they maintained the right appearances.

But not all my informal networks were as straightforward as Joy's kindness. Kathy, Kurt's wife and our next-door neighbor, provided a different kind of education in human nature.

She was always working on a pond in her backyard. It became my favorite refuge outside of Lola's house. The water was alive with tadpoles, fish, and frogs, a miniature ecosystem that seemed to operate on rules that made sense.

"Can I help?" I'd ask when I saw her working on some new project.

"Sure," she'd say, handing me tools or explaining what she was trying to accomplish.

Kathy tore apart her driveway and repoured the concrete herself, built an elaborate trellis for her climbing plants, then decided she needed to add onto her house. The addition required excavating the basement, and she hired me and three other neighborhood kids for what seemed like an incredible fortune: $1.25 per hour.

For a month, we dug through clay and rocks, our hands blistered and backs aching but motivated by the promise of real money for our labor. I calculated my earnings obsessively–hours worked multiplied by hourly wage, minus taxes that Kathy assured us she'd handle properly.

"You kids are working so hard," she'd say, bringing us lemonade while we sweated in the hole that was becoming her new basement. "I really appreciate this."

When the job was finally finished, when the last wheelbarrow of dirt had been hauled up from the excavation, I knocked on Kathy's door to collect my earnings. Instead of payment, I got a cheerful announcement.

"I've decided to throw a barbecue at the park for everyone instead of paying wages," she said, as if this was a generous upgrade to our original agreement. "Won't that be more fun than money?"

Standing on her doorstep, looking at the smile on her face while she explained why she wouldn't be honoring our agreement, I felt something cold and hard settle in my chest. This wasn't different from my parents' broken promises about Christmas lists or Playboy subscriptions. This was the same pattern: adults making commitments they never intended to keep, then acting like victims were ungrateful for questioning the betrayal.

"But you promised to pay us," I said, my voice steadier than I felt.

"Well, sometimes plans change," she replied. "The barbecue will be much more fun. You'll see."

I didn't go to the barbecue. I talked with the other kids and we all agreed not to go. The lesson was too important to dilute with free hamburgers and forced celebration.

Kathy had taught me that even adults who seemed different, who built interesting things and treated kids like capable workers, could be fundamentally dishonest when it served their interests.

The pattern was becoming unmistakable: watch what people do when they think the consequences don't matter. That's when you see who they really are.

The Retreat Begins

By sixth grade, I was becoming seriously quiet and withdrawn. Music, which I'd always enjoyed, became impossible because I couldn't hear where my parents were over the sound. It became critically important to know when they were approaching so I could bury myself in some hobby and become invisible.

I've never regained my ability to enjoy music. Even now, I only listen to it in the car to drown out traffic noise.

But during those elementary years, I'd learned something crucial about human relationships. David's calm household had shown me that not all families operated in constant chaos. Chris's situation taught me that physical abuse could be worse than mental abuse, but also that some kids were heading toward predictable disasters. The rock-hunting trips proved that even damaged adults could sometimes share genuine moments of connection.

The gregarious, happy child was disappearing, replaced by someone who found safety in solitude and systematic thinking. I buried myself deeper in hobbies, spent more time alone in my room, learning to move through the house like a ghost when the arguing started.

Even as I was withdrawing from the world, those elementary years had taught me something crucial about human relationships.

Chapter 7: Family Business Hell

You're My Slave

"Load those A-frames," Dad said one Saturday morning, gesturing toward the wooden display structures he'd built in the garage. He never said "please" or "thank you".

I jumped up eagerly. Finally, a chance to be part of something that mattered to him, to contribute more than just carrying supplies or fetching tools.

"I want to help," I said. "Really help. Not just carry stuff."

Dad stopped loading and looked at me with that expression that meant I'd said something wrong.

"You're my son and you're my slave," he said, his voice flat and matter of fact. "I own you, and you'll do exactly what I tell you to do. Nothing more, nothing less."

The words hit me like a physical blow. Slave. Property. Owned.

I stood there holding an A-frame, feeling something cold and heavy settle in my chest. This wasn't about wanting help with his art career. This was about power, control, making sure I understood exactly where I stood in his hierarchy.

I carried the A-frames to the station wagon in sullen silence, my excitement about participating replaced by that familiar sense of being reduced to a tool, a possession that existed solely for his convenience.

This was around fifth grade, when my parents discovered their business model that would eventually support them for decades. They'd bought the station wagon specifically for hauling Dad's artwork to weekend shows, and Dad had spent weeks in the garage building professional-looking display structures.

The irony wasn't lost on me, even at ten years old. Dad was an artist–someone who was supposed to understand beauty, creativity, the value of human expression. Yet he could look at his own child and see nothing but unpaid labor.

The Weekend Grind

Oceanside, Big Bear, Lake Arrowhead–we drove to dozens of public events where Dad would set up his displays and Mom would handle the customer interactions. Weekend after weekend, loading and unloading paintings, setting up easels, watching tourists examine his work with polite interest that sometimes translated into actual sales.

The routine was always the same. Friday evening, we'd spend hours loading the station wagon like we were packing for an expedition. Dad's paintings wrapped in blankets, easels broken down into pieces, boxes of supplies that might be needed for any conceivable situation. The back of that wagon became a carefully organized mobile gallery that smelled like turpentine and wood stain.

"Careful with that one," Dad would bark as I maneuvered a large canvas toward the car. "You almost dropped it."

Saturday morning meant getting up before dawn to drive to whatever town was hosting the art fair. Spending hours in the car locked in, without air conditioning, listening to my parents rehashing the same arguments about money. My sister and I were relegated to the cramped back seat with boxes of art supplies digging into our ribs.

"Did you remember the cash box?" Mom would ask for the fifth time.

"Of course, I remembered the cash box," Dad would snap back. "Do you think I'm an idiot?"

"I'm just checking. We can't afford to forget anything important."

"I'm not stupid."

The setup process was chaotic and unplanned. I stuffed A-frames and painting in the car, we drove to the location, then I unloaded everything and set them up. There was no plan, no pattern, no instruction.

"Richard, hold this steady while I adjust the legs," he'd command, treating me like a slightly more useful version of a clamp.

I learned to anticipate his needs, to position myself where I'd be most helpful, to stay invisible when customers approached. My role was to be instantly available for manual labor while remaining completely unobtrusive during the actual selling process.

The money wasn't huge—a portrait here, a landscape there, maybe a few hundred dollars on a good weekend. But it was real money, cash that, ironically, got us further in debt and more behind on the bills.

The Pressure Builds

But I was watching something else unfold. As their business success grew, so did their desperation to make it work.

The pressure of trying to make art pay the bills was already changing Dad. His artistic talent, which had once been a source of pride and escape, was becoming another source of stress. Every weekend show became a test of their family's financial survival. Every painting that didn't sell represented food we couldn't buy, bills we couldn't pay.

"We need to sell at least three pieces this weekend," he'd mutter while arranging his display.

The art that had once brought him joy was now weighed with desperate financial necessity. I watched him become increasingly stressed, more anxious about customer reactions, and more prone to explosive anger when things didn't go according to plan.

"Why aren't people buying?" he'd demand during the drive home from a slow weekend. "What's wrong with them?"

"Maybe it's the economy," Mom would suggest, trying to defuse his building rage.

"The economy's fine. People are just stupid. They'd rather buy mass-produced garbage than support real artists."

I learned to make myself invisible during these post-show debriefs during the long ride home, shrinking into the corner of the back seat while my parents dissected every interaction, every missed opportunity, every sign that their financial salvation might be slipping away.

The Human Pack Mule

My role in this enterprise was strictly manual labor. Load the car, unload the car, carry this, hold that, stay out of the way when real customers appeared. I was a pack mule with the additional burden of being able to understand exactly how little I mattered to the operation.

"Richard, bring me that red painting from the car," Dad would call out during setup.

"Which red painting?"

"The one with the cardinal. Use your brain."

I'd sprint to the car, locate the painting, and carry it back to him as quickly as possible. Any delay, any confusion, any failure to anticipate his needs would result in public humiliation disguised as instruction.

"Not that one, the other one. Can't you tell a cardinal from a robin? Pay attention to what you're doing."

The customers would smile sympathetically while I endured these corrections, probably thinking they were witnessing normal father-son interactions rather than systematic degradation designed to maintain absolute control.

Between the loading and unloading, there were many moments of sheer boredom after everything was set up. I'd sit behind the displays, playing quiet games or reading books, always aware that any noise or distraction could trigger Dad's fury.

"If I hear so much as a whisper from you while I'm talking to customers…" he'd warn us before each show.

The consequences were never specified, but we both understood the implications. Dad's belt, applied with careful precision in whatever private space was available.

The Slave's Perspective

As the weekends accumulated and the modest success continued, my parents became increasingly convinced that this was their path to financial freedom. Dad's government salary felt increasingly inadequate compared to the potential earnings from art sales.

They didn't share any details about their business with me, a mere child. I'd learned to tune out their arguments, lest they drive me insane, by daydreaming or pretending to sleep.

Their arguments and constant bickering forced me to withdraw into myself. That became a problem that I would fight for the rest of my life. A survival mechanism became so ingrained and automatic that throughout life I found it difficult to focus on anything for any length of time.

From my position as unpaid labor, I had a unique view of how the business functioned. I didn't see the money or their finances; they never shared details about those, but I saw the vast effort and time they were expending. One thing stood out to me: there was no planning; decisions were made instantly without research.

I watched customers walk by Dad's artwork without stopping, or they would stop to look but leave without buying anything.

I'd tuned out so much that I have only fragmentary memories of these expeditions to art shows. Mostly, I remember disrespect, forced labor, arguing, and the ever-present threat of the belt.

The Inevitable Escalation

By the time I reached sixth grade, the art business had consumed my parents' entire worldview, and the crisis with Mom had made everything worse. Every decision was filtered through its potential impact on their artistic careers while I walked on eggshells, terrified that any normal childhood behavior might trigger another catastrophe. Vacations became scouting trips for new shows.

I watched them transform from people who enjoyed art into people who were desperate for money. The joy of creation was being replaced by the anxiety of commerce, and that anxiety was making Dad even more controlling and explosive.

The "you're my slave" declaration wasn't an isolated incident–it was part of a pattern that got worse as the stakes got higher. Every weekend show became a family emergency that required total commitment from all of us, regardless of our own interests or needs.

"This is our livelihood," Dad would remind us before each trip. "Don't embarrass your mom."

The weight of that responsibility was crushing. My sister and I weren't just children accompanying our parents on business trips–we were potential liabilities who could damage their reputation if we failed to perform our roles perfectly.

I was learning that financial pressure could transform people in ways that success never could. The modest income from weekend art shows was creating more stress in our household than the steady poverty of Dad's government salary ever had.

But I was also absorbing lessons that would serve me decades later: how desperation could cloud business judgment, how success could create its own form of prison, and how important it was to maintain multiple income streams rather than betting everything on a single opportunity.

If I packed my mind in labeled boxes, I could find myself later.

Chapter 8: Little Mountain

Scouting a Life

The summer before junior high, our weekend art shows turned into scouting runs. Idlewild, Big Bear, Lake Arrowhead, Blue Jay, Lake Gregory. We still packed canvases and the metal money box, but the drives stretched, and every lookout became a place to try on a life.

"We could put the studio here," Mom said at a turnout above the lake. She traced the air, sketching rooms on the horizon. "Morning light from there. Storage along that wall."

They started close to home. Most San Bernardino listings blurred into beige and low walls. One did not. On Little Mountain, south of Stoddard Street, a realtor with a jangling bracelet led us into a strange honeycomb.

"Fifty bedrooms," she said. "It was built by a Mormon a hundred years ago. One room for each wife."

I don't know if that was a story she made up or truth. But it sounded romantic to my parents.

There was a kitchen as wide as a cafeteria. The hallway was so long that the light thinned out before it ended.

"We'd share it," Mom said. "A community."

"Whose rules?" Dad asked, palm on the banister as if it could answer.

I clapped once in a room the size of a classroom. The echo came back thin. I pictured waking up at night and not knowing which door led anywhere.

On the drive home, the mountain slid into the rearview like a ship we'd just left. At a red light, Dad said, "It's a no."

Mom let out the breath she'd been holding. "Yes. A no."

The search kept going. Weeks became months, then a lifestyle. My sister and I weren't briefed. We were the crew. Lift the crates. Carry the frames. Load the car. Smile at browsers. Pack in the cold. Move when told. Adjust fast.

The Mountain Commute

When the hunt stalled, they opened a shop in Blue Jay. It was a small space in a large building, like a strip mall. Dad hung his graphics and paintings in the window.

The commute cut the day into blocks you could count. Pre-dawn loading under the carport light. Breath hanging like smoke. The Rim Road's switchbacks tipping your stomach just enough to remind you where you were. In winter, the turnout ritual to chain the tires.

"Gloves," Dad said, and I handed them over. Chain clinked over cold pavement. I fed it under the tire while he rolled the car a foot at a time. Jaw set. Cheeks raw from wind. The metal smell lodged in your nose and stayed.

On the way up, arguments tried to resolve themselves.

"You under-ordered frames," Mom said at a red light, receipts fanned across her lap.

"They're backordered," he said.

"You could have checked earlier."

"I did."

Green. We moved. Some days it was words. Some days, it was the absence of words. Silence had mass. I watched the pressure like weather. When to look out the window. When a question would be kindling.

At the shop we swept, Windexed, squared tags. Dad straightened paintings until they sat true. Mom adjusted the display, stepped back, tilted her head, nudged a piece an inch, then another.

Blue Jay sits at around three to four thousand feet. Winter there looks friendly. Snow on roofs by morning, gone by afternoon. Plows leave small ridges kids kick apart on the way to school. Mountain life seems manageable. Go higher, and winter stops pretending. We weren't there yet.

Days narrowed into a loop. Open. Smile. Explain. Wrap. Count. Lock. Drive down through trees and headlights, chains tapping the wheel wells in a steady rhythm you can't turn off.

Distance and Fossils

Even Mom saw the distance Dad kept, especially from me.

"He should take you out," she said one night, drying a plate while he read at the table. "A hike. You like rocks."

"I like fossils," I said.

"Perfect," she said, a little louder. "Take him to Little Mountain."

He folded the paper along the crease and set it down. "Put your shoes on."

We parked at the base where chain-link tried to keep no one out. The trail climbed through scrub oak and between boulders that looked like sleeping animals. He walked at a pace that allowed talking without requiring it.

I slid a putty knife into a shale seam and eased it until the rock lifted in thin pages. A faint fern appeared, delicate as a pencil line trapped between layers.

"I found one," I said, turning it to the light, so the ribs showed.

He glanced, expression unchanged. "Uh-huh." Hands in pockets, he waited while I followed a lizard darting between the rocks. I grabbed its tail, which snapped off so it could get away.

I pried a few more sheets. "That's a bedding plane," I said, hearing my certainty. "The shale splits clean if you hit it right."

He watched. No agreement. No argument. Instruction without invitation. I took what there was and made it mine.

Back home, Mom met us in the doorway. "Well?"

"We found shale," I said, lifting the bag.

She smiled at me and then looked at him. He shrugged. She sighed and let it go. I lined the pieces on my dresser like a small museum. The fern went in front.

The Pinewood Derby

Shandin Hills sent home a flyer with a cartoon race car and a bold line near the top: Fathers must enter with their sons. I set it on the dinner table.

"They made it a rule," I said. "Can't race without you."

Dad read the headline, then the fine print, then the fee. He pulled three singles from his wallet and set them down like paying a toll because you need the bridge. "We'll build it Saturday."

We opened the kit on the kitchen table. The pine block felt heavier than it looked. He rolled it in his palm, examined the grain, and drew a faint line with a carpenter's pencil.

"I'll Cut along that," he said. "Long wedge. Weight in the back."

"Like a shark," I said.

He nodded, "Just be quiet and stay out of my way. These tools are sharp."

A sound that might have been a laugh. The handsaw tugged and sang. I watched while he cut, then worked sandpaper until my fingertips tingled and the floor warmed with sawdust. He taped two pennies near the rear, smoothed the tape with his thumb, and spun a wheel on a nail to check for wobble.

"Axles straight," he said. "You want smooth."

We didn't talk much. Not tense. Not easy. He gave it a couple hours and then rinsed the dust from his hands like a man who'd reached the natural end of a task.

Race day smelled like floor wax and buttered popcorn. The track rose from the stage and ran bright down the multipurpose room. Fathers clustered and traded words like graphite and alignment. At check-in, a kid whispered, "That one's plain," as if plain were a sin.

We drew lane three. Dad stood behind me, not touching, not far. The starter set the gate. The room settled.

"Ready."

The brace dropped. Fast cars streaked and became sound. Ours rolled. Not broken, not stuck–just slow. The squeak of our axles caught the room's attention. By the time our car tapped the bumper, winners were already collecting high fives.

Heat climbed up my neck. I nodded at nothing and kept my mouth shut. Dad rested his hand on my shoulder for a beat, then let it fall.

"Let's go," he said.

"There are more races," I said, softer than I meant to.

He met my eyes and shook his head once. "We're done for today."

Outside, the light felt brighter than it should have. We walked to the car without speaking. When the door shut, he finally said, "Being slow isn't something to cry over." Not hard. Tired.

"I'm not," I said. It wasn't exactly tears. It was something heavier I couldn't name.

At home, I set the car on the dresser next to the fossil fern. Side by side they made a language. One a record of pressure and time. The other a lesson in drag and weight. I rolled the car along the dresser's edge until the squeak smoothed for a few inches, then left it pointing nowhere in particular.

The Purge

I always found it odd how much my mother identified with me. I never knew what to make of it. My interests felt like hers, my wins like hers, my losses too. When I changed, she felt betrayed.

A few days after the Pinewood Derby, I stood over my rock collection. Trays, labels, the shine of polished agate, the chalky dull of sandstone. I lifted a tray and poured it into a trash bag. The clatter sounded like breaking dishes. Another tray. Another clatter. My mother later said a teacher must have turned me against it. That was not true. Most of the rocks came from trips with my father or shows where he bought them for me. They were pieces of him in my room. I wanted them gone.

It was the Pinewood Derby. The school intended this to be a bonding moment between fathers and sons. My dad, instead, put in the bare minimum by himself while I watched. We lost because he didn't care–he was just going through the motions.

I had four cores from drilling, smooth cylinders with their own rings of time. I made sure those went into the trash. He had stolen them from work and handed them to me like a prize. Out they went.

When she found out, her voice broke. "Why would you do that?" The question was not about rocks. It was about her, and the part of herself she had parked in me.

I had no safe answer. I kept moving. A few specimens slipped the purge; none of those originated with my dad. I still have them. The rest went out with the trash, heavy and final.

It was a gorgeous collection of several hundred pieces. And they were poisoned, the ugliest things I owned.

Working for "Family"

By fall, the shop needed more hands, or that was the argument. Mom stood in my doorway with the store ledger tucked under her arm.

"You're old enough to help," she said. "Families pitch in."

"What's the pay?" I asked.

She smiled as if I'd tossed a joke into the room. "It's family. We don't pay family."

"You taught me to work for money," I said. "Chores for allowance. Jobs for cash. I'm sticking with that."

"Don't be difficult. We need you."

"I'm not working the shop for free," I said. Flat and steady.

Color rose into her cheeks. "You're being selfish."

"I deserve to be paid," I said.

She looked at the empty shelf where the Pinewood car and the rock collection had previously sat. It was now filled with science fiction paperbacks.

"Fine," she said. "Do your homework."

I didn't clock a single hour at the Blue Jay shop. Not one. The line held.

The lesson my parents drilled into me about doing chores for an allowance stuck with me my whole life. I don't work for free.

When Home Turned Unbearable

By winter, the house carried a low hum that didn't quit. Not loud. Persistent. Arguments started in the kitchen and condensed on everything. Frames that hadn't arrived. Deposits that hadn't cleared. Nine versus ten o'clock opening. Whether we should be looking for a house at all.

"You didn't call the supplier," Mom said, flipping a receipt with her fingernail.

"I called every day this week," Dad said, keeping his voice level. "They're shipping Tuesday."

"You always say Tuesday."

"Because that's what they say."

Cabinet doors closed harder than needed. The heater clicked on and off like it had an opinion. The dog watched from the doorway, waiting for instructions that didn't come. I learned the indicators. A certain rattle from the plates meant it would blow over. A certain quiet meant it wouldn't.

Teenage arrived on its own schedule. Jeans went short in a month. My voice cracked mid-sentence in English and a girl in the front row turned and smiled without malice, which somehow stung more. My skin tried new topographies across my forehead. I bought deodorant with chore money and used it like insurance because the locker room punished a single mistake.

Some nights I slept like a stone and woke heavy, standing in the kitchen in the dark with a glass of milk, listening to the house breathe. On other nights, I lay awake and counted the spaces between their sentences down the hall. When the front door opened too hard after closing, my body flinched before my brain caught up. I started getting up early to draw quiet into me before the day claimed it.

I built routines because routines held. A stack of library books thick enough to be a wall. Eggs flipped clean because a small win counted. Backpack staged by the door at night, pencils sharp, paper squared, even if what sat inside wouldn't impress anyone.

Sometimes Mom tried to draft me into the fight.

"Tell your father what he does," she said, voice bright and brittle. "Tell him how he talks to you."

I kept my tone level. "I need to finish an assignment." I stepped out of the blast radius.

"Don't walk away from me, young man," she said.

"I'll be in my room," I said, and left. She really wanted me to confront Dad? Did I look stupid or something?

When the kitchen got loud, I went to the backyard with a basketball. The hoop had no net. The backboard was crooked just enough that the ball came off at an angle unless I hit the sweet spot. Thud, slap, thud, slap, until my breathing evened and the dog lay down by the fence and sighed. Cold crept through my sweatshirt. The noise loosened.

None of it felt like tragedy. It had become normal. I didn't announce a philosophy. I practiced one. Less talk, more angles. Less heat, more distance. Catch the first flicker of a fight and step aside. Learn which doors close quietly. Remain quiet. Keep enough distance from Dad that he couldn't reach me.

And I didn't trust Mom at all. Whatever love she'd had for me when I was small had been absorbed by the gallery, the arguments, the depression, the business. By high school it was simply gone. Not hostile — just absent. I was furniture to her too, by then, just quieter furniture than I was to him.

Shandin Hills

Shandin Hills Junior High School sprawled at the base of Little Mountain, long and low, glass and brick that looked newer than it felt after a week. The halls smelled of carpet glue and floor wax. Lockers slammed like a drumline warming up. Rumors ran ahead of the bell. Fights last week. Police are in the lot. A teacher stabbed. True or not, the idea shaped how people moved.

Every day one I chose a seat close to the door. Close enough to leave without looking like I wanted to.

A boy in a brown jacket sat behind me. "You new?"

"Yeah."

"You got a quarter?"

"No."

He snorted. "You will."

He was wrong. I learned the angles. Which teachers watched the hall. Which doors stuck. Which corners turned into bottlenecks. I moved like I had a destination even when I didn't.

Classes felt like a radio caught between stations. If something mattered, I could lock on for hours. Worksheets didn't. The bell landed clean.

Some teachers cut through the static. In Shop, Mr. Wyckoff kept his sleeves rolled and the rules clear.

"You drop it, you push it," he said, tapping his boot on concrete. "Drop and give me fifty."

A red resin rose popped from my mold, skittered, and pinged off a table leg.

"Floor," he said without looking up.

I dropped and counted. Sawdust and machine oil in the air. At twenty-five, my arms trembled and then settled. At fifty, I stood.

"Trim the edges," he said. "Try again."

Not personal. Just rules. I respected that.

In another room, clay waited under plastic. The kiln glowed behind wire, heat rolling off it in sheets. My bowls came out lopsided and honest. Warm in my hands. Soft into hard. Shapeless into form. That made sense.

I ate outside when I could. The low wall by the courtyard gave me a read of the board. Which groups radiated risk. Which teachers could settle a crowd with a look. By October I had a route that kept me clear. By December I knew which raised voice meant stop and which meant move.

Money, Purchases, and Patterns

Home ran hot. The shop and the hunt consumed oxygen. Money was tight or about to be tight. Mom brought home boxes with catalogs and party scripts that promised bonuses if you hit numbers.

"Tupperware pays extra if I do five," she said, pointing at lid diagrams like they were maps.

"Avon does too," I said, tapping lipstick samples lined like a parade.

She laughed without humor. "We're diversified."

When her mood dropped, Dad brought home something you could place. A chair. A carved chest. Sometimes jewelry. He set it down like an apology you could dust.

"This is maple," he said once, pleased by dovetail joints you could admire from across the room. "Solid."

"It's beautiful," she said, and for an hour the house went calm. Then the calm thinned. The furniture stayed. If he had stopped buying, half their problems might have evaporated overnight. But it helped with Mom's depression for a time.

I was taking notes without meaning to. Years later, when fog slid in on me, I tried the same fix. Shopping sprees that lit the brain for an hour and left a bill under your ribs for months. Debt growing every month until it became unbearable.

What I Learned

If junior high had a headline for me, it wasn't chaos. It was calibration. I learned to introvert and give distance because people proved dangerous and unreliable, often enough to make distance the safest move.

The distance wasn't emptiness. It was position. I read rooms fast. I chose angles. I caught the first signs of trouble and stepped aside before the wave hit. On paper, I didn't excel. In practice, I built a toolkit that kept me upright.

On Little Mountain, I split shale and pocketed a fern that outlived everything. In Shandin's halls, I learned to move without drawing fire. At home, I learned to keep my own weather when the forecast never changed.

By spring, the year felt like a slope under my shoes. The system taught one thing. My life required another. I kept the skills that worked. I kept my balance. And when it was time to move, I moved.

I stayed a step ahead so I didn't have to look back.

Somewhere in junior high the report card envelope stopped mattering.

Not because I stopped worrying about it. Because my parents stopped looking. The gallery was eating everything by then — their time, their arguments, their attention. I'd set the envelope on the kitchen table and it would sit there for days. Eventually it disappeared, filed or thrown away, and no one said a word either way.

I didn't feel relief. I felt something I couldn't name yet: I didn't exist enough to be worth checking on.

The thing that had kept me working — fear of what happened if I didn't — was gone. I couldn't make myself care about assignments that meant nothing in a house that had stopped functioning as a family. My grades started to slip. Not dramatically at first. Just enough to notice, if anyone had been noticing. No one was.

Chapter 9: High School Hell

I had checked out. Not from any single moment but from everything — gradually and then completely, the way a house goes dark one room at a time. High school happened to me. College happened to me. I was present for the logistics and absent for the rest. If these chapters feel more distant than what came before, that's not an accident. That's what it was like.

By the end of high school I didn't care whether I lived or died. Not suicidal — I wasn't making plans. Just empty. The part of me that was supposed to want things had gone quiet.

The Christmas Vow

We drove down to Escondido for Christmas to see the grandparents. Their house smelled of pine cleaner and ham glaze. Wrapping paper crackled underfoot. In the middle of the living room, my father cleared his throat and smiled like a performance was coming.

"I can't wait until you bring a girl home," he said, squeezing my shoulder as if pinning me in place. "You, mister secret-keeper. You think she won't find out? I'm going to tell her everything about you. Every stupid thing you've ever done, every night you cried, all those times you peed in bed. Every messy little habit you try to hide."

He leaned closer, breathing sharply with coffee. "Remember those naked pictures I took when you were little? I'm showing them to her. I want her to see exactly who you are."

Thin laughter fluttered, brittle as ornament glass. Ham glaze hung sweet and turned my stomach. Blood roared in my ears. The carpet's blue flowers smeared as the room tunneled. I locked my knees and kept my face blank. Any expression was ammunition. Any backtalk brought the belt.

No one cared. This was normal for him. They ignored it. No one looked up. No one said a word. No one stepped between us.

He patted my back twice, the practiced weight of it. My skin crawled as a six-year-old memory stirred and went dark. He turned away.

Heat climbed my throat until it felt like swallowing fire. Words hammered against my teeth. You will not get that chance. I swallowed them whole, tasting copper. Something inside me splintered, then sealed shut, cold and final.

Right there, amid pine cleaner and blinking lights, I laid down a silent vow. I would never bring any woman into his reach. I carried that vow for decades, heavy and unbroken. He knew what he was doing. He wasn't being clumsy or cruel for the sport of it. He was making sure I would never get close enough to anyone to talk.

He kept smiling, basking in uneasy chuckles, his bitter point hitting home. I learned to breathe shallow, to angle my shoulders out of his grasp, and to store hurt where his stories could not find it.

I wanted to cry but knew better.

Moving

"We are moving to Lake Arrowhead," my father said, not looking up from the bills spread across the kitchen table. His voice made it sound like weather, something that happened to everyone and no one at the same time.

My sister and I were not asked. We were told.

Mom stood by the sink, wiping an already clean counter. The sponge squeaked against the tile. She tried on a smile that did not fit. "It will be quieter up there," she said, as if promising herself a soft place to land. "Better for the gallery. Better for all of us."

Dad stacked the envelopes and squared the corners with his thumbs. "The commute is killing us," he said. "Decision is made."

There was nothing I could say or do. Compliance cost less than open war. Who knows, it might be a good thing.

Heat climbed my neck. I kept my hands under the table so no one would see them tremble. A dozen arguments rushed to my mouth, crowded together, then fell back. I had learned the rules. Do not challenge the verdict. Do not ask for reasons he does not want to give.

"Anything specific you want?" he said, glancing at me like a foreman checking a clipboard. "Speak up if you have something practical."

I swallowed. Practical. Keep it small. Keep it safe. "I just want space for my plywood board," I said. "The model railroad. A hobby room or a big bedroom. That is all."

Dad nodded once, transaction noted. "Basement will do."

Mom turned, hope lighting her face for a second. "We can make it nice," she said, too bright. "Shelves. Good light. You will have room to spread out."

I nodded as if I believed it. Inside, something pinched tight, the way you brace before a shot. I wanted to say I do not want a new house; I want a safe one. I wanted to say, ask me. Instead, I said, "Okay."

Dad pushed back his chair. The legs scraped the floor. "Good," he said, as if we had just completed a productive meeting.

Mom rinsed the sponge until the water ran cold, eyes shining more than she wanted them to. My sister stared at her cereal, spoon idle, like she had learned the same lesson I had. Silence keeps the peace that never comes.

I folded the want back into myself, neat as a letter you are not sending. Outside, a breeze moved through the trees. Inside, the decision sat where it landed, heavy as a hammer still warm from use.

I wondered if I would make any friends.

We moved the next day. Apparently, the decision had been made long before the dining room discussion. The consultation with me and my sister a sham.

I never had a chance to say goodbye to my friends. One day I had friends, the next I lived in a new house, alone with my sister.

The House on the Hill

They had already opened the gallery in Blue Jay. The commute ate time and gas and frayed tempers. By dinner, they were worn thin.

"We cannot keep doing this drive," Dad said, rubbing his temples as spaghetti steamed up from our chipped plates. "It is stupid. We are moving up the mountain."

Mom nodded too fast. "It will be quieter," she said, twisting a napkin into a rope. "Better for the gallery. Better for us."

"Better for my sanity," he snapped, then softened it with a sigh.

The room smelled like sauce and tired people. I kept my eyes on the red swirl in my bowl and chewed without tasting.

Sometime in that stretch he quit Norton. There was no speech. Just a slammed door, a box of art books on the kitchen floor, and voices scraping against each other late into the night.

"I hate the politics," he said. "These officers, all they do is take. They are corrupt."

"It is a paycheck," Mom answered, quiet and firm. "We need it until the gallery stands on its own."

"Then it better stand," he said, and the house held the echo.

By the time boxes stacked along the hallway, the place sounded like a drum when anyone walked.

They chose a three-story place in Lake Arrowhead Villas, a few miles from the Village. Pines crowded the road, sap sweet in the afternoon heat. The house was built into the slope like a fist pressed into wet clay and left to dry.

Dad worked the new front door key. The latch gave with a hollow click. Cool air and varnish met us.

"This is it," he said, satisfied, as if the house were an answer.

The lowest level was half buried. That became the family room. We wrestled a massive console against the wall, television, record player, and radio in glossy wood, a low electric hum as it warmed. A couch faced it, cushions already giving up in the middle.

A short hall led to a small bathroom and a smaller bedroom. That one was mine. The air down there held a clean chill and a thread of earth. When I opened the window, pine breath slipped in and mixed with mineral cold from the hill.

I looked around, checking for exits. My bedroom bothered me; the only way out was through the door leading into the family room. There was a window, but it would probably kill me to jump from that height.

Below my room sat the basement, a Yankee cellar. One wall pressed into the hillside. The other ran the length of the house in stacked, rough block. The air felt older down there, damp and metallic, like pennies and wet stone. A single chain hung from the bare bulb. Pull, click, small circle of light. Dust motes lifted like slow snow.

The floor was poured concrete that sloped toward a rusted drain. The furnace ticked as it cooled, a patient animal at rest. When the wind pushed, the vent rattled and the whole space answered with a low hum.

My cat discovered the heater early and spent most of the days for years sleeping on top of the fiberglass insulation. Cats like to be warm, and you couldn't do better than that space.

I traced the line from my bed to the stairs to the back door and timed it in my head. Door latch, two steps to the hall, eight down to the cellar, twelve across to the basement door if I had to. I tested it once, and it groaned like a warning. Good to know. Not plan A.

Back upstairs, I cracked the bedroom window anyway, just enough to let the hill breathe into the room. Pine, sap, a hint of cold dirt. I set my shoes side by side under the bed, soles facing out, laces loose, and slid a small flashlight into the nightstand. Habit. Map the room. Stage the exits. Then I lay back and watched the ceiling until my eyes learned the pattern of the plaster and the house settled around me like a big, creaking animal that, for the moment, meant me no harm.

I was still counting routes when Dad's boots hit the stairs. He thumped the plasterboard walls with his knuckles. "Plenty of room down here for your hobby."

I nodded, listening to the furnace tick as it cooled, breathing the mix of cold soil and hot dust.

The second floor held the formal living room and kitchen. The living room wore its best clothes. Mom set out glass birds with careful fingers, lined up porcelain dogs, arranged small knickknacks until they caught the square of afternoon light. "Do not touch," she said, smiling without looking at me. The carpet ran smooth and new under my socks. The kitchen was bright and loud with tile. Every footstep gave a sharp reply. Lemon cleaner bit my nose.

The top floor matched the living room's footprint and became my parents' bedroom. A smaller side room, same size as mine, became my sister's. Another bathroom sat off the hall.

We walked the whole place once, our steps echoing up and down the stairwells. I kept my eyes open for exits and hazards. The two fireplaces bothered me most, one on the first floor and one on the second. Just outside, pressed to the chimney, a huge pine leaned in, its branches overhanging the top. Pine, pitch, dry needles. As far as I know, my parents never used those fireplaces, and that felt like luck.

"Well?" Dad asked, halfway between floors, hand on the rail.

"Lot of stairs," I said.

"Good for your legs," he answered, already moving.

Mom brushed my sleeve as she passed. "We will make it home," she whispered, hopeful and already a little tired.

I kept my thoughts folded tight. The house smelled like fresh paint and new promises. Under it, I heard old sounds, the hum of machines, the space where arguments could roll down the stairs and land hard.

A year later, two men backed a truck up, carried in slate like tombstones, leveled the table, stretched the green felt, chalked the cues.

Dad racked the balls with a rare smile. "Eight ball. Break."

They played for two evenings, the clack of balls clean as a metronome. By the third week, envelopes and magazines drifted onto the felt, then laundry. The table went quiet.

I never understood why they bought a pool table. It was an enormous expense, and, after the first few days, they never played the game.

Later, during a trip to the desert, Mom found an old popcorn machine, about the size of a refrigerator. It looked like it had been retired from a carnival or something. She placed it proudly against one wall, and it soon became yet another expensive toy that was never used. It was too hard to clean after each use.

The Board Falls

That board had taken years. Nine feet by five, built on plywood in my bedroom in San Bernardino, with plaster mountains, hand-painted rock faces, hundreds of feet of track, trees no taller than my thumbnail planted one by one, buildings scratch-built from balsa and cardboard. One locomotive that I knew every inch of. My friends and I would set up elaborate war games on it — armies moving through the mountain passes, battles fought around the rail lines, hours gone before anyone noticed. It was the one place where something I'd built mattered to someone besides me.

When it came time to move it, we tilted it on its side to get it through the door.

The plaster mountains let go first, sliding like snow off a roof. The track lifted in a curling sheet, then tore. Tiny trees popped free with sharp little sounds. Buildings I'd spent entire weekends on dropped and shattered. The whole thing came down in slow motion and then all at once, years of work in a chalky heap on the floor.

My chest went tight. For half a second I almost made a sound. I swallowed it, knelt down, picked up a few pieces, then got the broom. My face stayed plain because my face was always plain when something important broke in front of them.

Neither parent said anything useful. No acknowledgment of what it had taken to build, or what it was. My father gestured toward the Yankee cellar in the new house — he'd actually factored it into choosing the place, space for Richard's hobby, look what we got you. "Plenty of room down there," he said. My mother said nothing. They loaded the pieces into a trash bag. I held the dustpan.

Belinda watched from the doorway. She didn't say anything either — she'd learned the same rule I had about keeping your face plain — but I saw her eyes go to the dustpan and back to me, and there was something in that look. She knew what it had meant. She was probably the only other person in that house who did.

I never used that cellar. Not once. I had no intention of building anything in that house. By the time we arrived, I already knew I wasn't staying any longer than I had to. The room they'd picked the house partly for sat empty the entire time we lived there.

I stood there with the broom and understood something I'd been circling for years. They hadn't destroyed the board on purpose. That was almost worse — it was just in the way, the same as I was. My father wasn't going to change. My mother was not going to protect me. I'd been tracking both of those as open questions. I closed them.

They weren't my parents. They were obstacles. One of them was dangerous.

I was too young to leave and my sister was too young to be left alone with them. But the moment I was old enough, I was gone. I stopped waiting and started building what I'd need to get out — a job, money, a car, a plan. Every shift I worked from that point on was a brick in the wall between me and this house.

Adolescence Without a Map

Adolescence slammed into me the way summer storms hit the mountain, loud, sudden, humming with static. No one explained anything. No talk about bodies changing, moods swinging, thoughts ricocheting. Just rules delivered like traffic tickets.

Dad laid them out at breakfast, the smell of burnt toast hanging in the air.

"Do this," he said, pointing his butter knife. "Be there. No backtalk."

Mom refilled my orange juice, eyes skittering between us. "Listen to your father."

Heat ran wild under my skin, a restless current I could not ground. My voice deepened without warning. Words cracked like dry branches. When I tried to joke, they called it attitude. When I fell silent, they called it sulking. If I said anything other than "Yes sir" I was called a smart ass.

Orders kept coming. Curfews, chores, a list of no's that grew longer by the week. "Shirt tucked. Hair off the ears. You answer when I speak." Each sentence felt like a collar tightening.

I took control in small ways. I stopped getting haircuts. Let it grow long, down to my belly button. I bought a chain with a marijuana leaf symbol hanging around my neck. I didn't even know what it symbolized. All I knew was it would piss off my parents. And for the record, I never used the drug (or any illicit drug for that matter) throughout my entire life.

My parents pretended not to notice.

One afternoon, hauling firewood up the back stairs, I muttered, "I am not a pack mule."

"What did you say?" he barked from the deck, sawdust still in his hair.

"Nothing," I snapped, too sharp, too fast.

He was down the stairs in two strides, eyes cold. "Watch that tone, young man."

My shoulders squared before I could stop them, a reflex, the body insisting it was bigger now. He noticed. For a heartbeat, the air between us crackled, my face grew hot. Then he turned away, a warning left hanging like a half-swung fist.

I was still their property.

Inside, muscles stretched, bones ached, hunger roared. I slept hard and woke harder, sheets twisted into knots. My thoughts sprinted ahead, then doubled back to bite. I mouthed off, stumbled, tried again. I carried the new weight in my bones like unfamiliar armor.

Mom studied me like a machine making a new noise. "Eat," she said, sliding an extra pork chop onto my plate. "You are growing." When my temper flared, she retreated, wiping counters already clean.

They seemed startled that change arrived on schedule, surprised that a quiet boy sprouted angles and opinions. Chore charts went on the fridge. Curfews in red. A note on my door that read Knock went unanswered. The rules landed on a kid morphing too fast to keep his balance, a kid without the language to say, this is not rebellion; it is becoming.

So, I poured the burn in my chest into reading and scrawled journals no one would ever read. Silence sometimes kept the peace. Sometimes it only made the echo louder.

Rim of the World

The timing of the move lined up with the start of high school. San Gorgonio High in San Bernardino felt like a threat. The street stories talked about fights, tension, gangs, and how fast things went wrong. Rim of the World High sat up here. Fewer fights. There was some drinking, and people looked the other way. About fifteen hundred students moved through those halls in waves.

I did not look forward to any of it. I wanted to get it over and done with. In junior high my attention had already split into a hundred pieces. I could not hold it even on things I liked.

When I was not in school, I shut my door and read. Paperback spines lined up like soldiers. Pages smelled faintly sweet and dusty. Books gave me a way to breathe.

My parents did not knock. They did not respect, or even acknowledge, my privacy. They came in and out as they pleased. Almost safe is not safe.

Property doesn't get privacy. It just gets used.

The Sewer Notices

Two years in, the city said the old cesspools had to go. Connect to the sewer. It made sense to me. Waste moved downhill. The lake sat below us, and the math did not care about feelings.

The notices arrived with deadlines and fees. The sewer line stopped a few yards from the house. The trenching and connection would be our responsibility. Thousands of dollars.

My parents ignored the letters. No one from the city came to enforce it. They bought bottles of additives and poured them into the toilets. It worked for a while. Years later, when I came back to visit, the first thing that hit me was the smell. Then, the black stains that haloed the bowls.

School Without Belonging

High school narrowed into a private corner I carried from class to class. I learned which lockers did not slam, which stairwell stayed quiet, which cafeteria table let me keep my back to the wall. I kept my head down and my mouth shut. The halls smelled like floor wax and wet denim on rainy days, like hot dust and perfume when the heaters kicked on. Bells rang, and kids surged like a tide I did not belong to.

At lunch I read. Paperbacks with cracked spines, library stamps fading at the edges. I opened a book and let the noise dull to a far hum, trays clattering, a laugh that cut like glass, sneakers squeaking on linoleum. I watched the clock because it promised an end to whatever class I was trapped in, even if the next one was no better. By the second week, I could map exits from every room without looking up, doors, windows, the angle of desks, pinch points in a crowd. My body sat in a chair. My mind traced escape routes.

"What are you even reading?" a boy asked once, shadow falling over my page.

"History," I said.

He snorted. "Nerd," and moved on. The word hit like a pebble, barely worth a flinch.

Criticism did not land in real time. I heard it and kept moving. The words slid past like rain on glass and left no mark, or so I thought. Minutes later, or days, or weeks, sometimes years, it circled back and hit. Hard. A delayed punch. I learned to treat it like weather: shelter first, then read the forecast when the sky cleared.

I did not know what I was supposed to learn besides compliance. Formulas slid off me. Essays came back with red marks that said vague without saying what sharp meant. Teachers spoke about the future like a bus everyone was catching next year. I could not see it. At home, the nights went long, and the air felt thin. I did not want to keep circling the same arguments and the same walls.

For a long time, I had no friends. Loneliness settled like a draft you cannot find, always there, making you fold your arms tighter.

My grades had collapsed and kept going. I'd kept B+, A- through grade school because I was terrified of what happened if I didn't. That fear was gone now — my parents were absorbed in the gallery and hadn't looked at a report card since junior high. Without the fear, I had nothing to replace it. I couldn't make myself focus on work that meant nothing to me, in classrooms run by teachers who wanted compliance, in a building I spent most of my time mapping for exits.

Teachers read it as attitude or laziness. A few said so directly. None of them asked what was happening at home. I wouldn't have told them if they had.

The system wanted me in line. I had run out of reasons to stand in it.

I dreamed of a nuclear war that would destroy the planet or a plague that would wipe out humanity.

The thoughts in my head grew dark and forbidding.

Fearsome Foursome

Dan told stories as if he was letting me in on a secret club. "Brian, Bob, Randy, us four," he said, counting on his knuckles. "We call it the Fearsome Foursome." He talked about hiking through the woods, hunting elves, Castle Park trips, nights that stretched until the clock forgot what day it was. He made it sound like a place where a kid like me could fit.

"Think I could join?" I asked one afternoon, half joking, half hoping.

"You are always welcome to hang," he said. "But the guys want it to stay four. Nothing personal."

Nothing personal landed like a small stone in my shoe, there every step. I avoided him for a few days, then let it go. I still showed up. Some of the shine was gone. Almost was still warmer than empty.

The first time I walked into Dan's mom's place, the smell hit me. Stale beer, warm smoke, something sour baked into the carpet. Empty bottles filled with cigarette ashes crowded every flat surface. Ashtrays overflowed in soft gray dunes. The TV glowed blue in the corner, sound low. A path through the living room snaked between cases of empty beer bottles and a leaning tower of pizza boxes. His mom was divorced and rarely around. The house felt abandoned in the way a party feels after it had gone on too long.

Brian lifted a bottle in salute. "You want one?"

"I am good," I said.

He shrugged and tipped it back. Cigarette ash fell on his jeans. He did not brush it away.

Randy cracked a window and took a drag like he was born doing it. "We are playing Risk later," he said. "Winner gets the couch."

Bob laughed from the kitchen. "Winner gets first pick of the warm beer."

We played games at Dan's kitchen table until the board blurred in the smoke. War of the Ring. Risk. Battles past midnight. I won more than my share, but it did not feel like winning in that room. Bottles piled up as if they were keeping score louder than the dice.

"Come on," Brian said, sliding a bottle toward me, foam slicking the rim. "Loosen up."

"I do not drink," I said.

"Suit yourself." He popped another cap, the metal pinging off a plate.

People changed after the third or fourth. Voices got elastic. Jokes turned mean. Time went soft. The laughter took on an edge that made my shoulders rise without me noticing. I kept my hands busy, moving pieces, tallying points, stacking cards, anything to keep from reaching for a bottle just to quiet the room's demand.

By the second month, the house had a permanent crunch underfoot, bits of glass, stale chips, old ash. The smell clung to my clothes. Outside, I opened my jacket and waved at the air before walking home.

"I like being around you guys," I told Dan once on the porch, breath fogging the cold. "I just do not want to drink."

He bumped my shoulder. "You do not have to," he said, and he meant it. Then he went back in, and the door breathed out smoke.

The heavier the drinking got, Brian and Dan leading, the more I felt myself pulled inward. The peer pressure was not a shove. It was a low tug, the way gravity wins if you stand too long. I ignored it because drunk people lose control.

I could not afford to lose control.

After a while, going over meant bracing. A clean shirt I did not mind sacrificing to the smell. A plan to sit near a cracked window. An excuse rehearsed in case the night started to boil. I showed up anyway. I wanted to belong to something. Anything.

Some nights the old rhythm held, dice and trash talk, maps spread out, the TV muttering to itself in the next room. Other nights I sat quietly at the edge of the mess, feeling the pull to disappear. The foursome stayed the foursome. I stayed almost in the room, invited, not inside the circle.

Years later, contact faded. Dan settled down, found religion, married, turned steady and likable. Brian went military, then computers. Bob and Randy vanished after graduation and never crossed my path again. What stayed with me was the sound of caps pinging on the table, the smell of ash in curtains, and the way a closed group can make you feel both chosen and turned away in the same breath.

I thought of them as my friends, but really, they were just people to hang out with. There was no friendship there.

First Jobs

When I turned seventeen, my father did not ask. He folded the evening paper, looked over the top of his glasses, and delivered it like a verdict. "It is time to work," he said. "You are getting a job."

Mom set down a potholder too carefully, the stove ticking as it cooled. I waited for the rest of the speech. There was none. It was not a conversation.

My first job lasted one day. Upholstery cleaning. The van smelled of wet fabric, soap, and old mildew. The boss drove with the window cracked and a cigarette burning low, ash trembling on the tip.

"Grab the hoses," he said, already moving. "Do not kink them."

We lugged gear up the apartment stairs, which were slick with cleaner. I lifted cushions, slid the wand along damp fabric, watched gray water run through clear tubing like secrets draining out of sofas. My forearms shook by noon. The machine's drone pressed into my skull. By evening, my clothes were clammy and my hands smelled like soap I would never use again.

"Twenty dollars," the boss said, peeling a bill and a crumpled ten from his pocket. "We will call you."

They did not. The silence told me everything.

The Lake Arrowhead liquor store hired me next. The doorbell chimed a flat note when it opened. The place smelled of varnished wood, cardboard, and the sweet bite of spilled whiskey.

Bill, my boss, had been a World War II Nazi U-boat commander, and he carried himself like a man who still liked giving orders. He spoke in short sentences, his eyes moving like a radar sweep.

I sat lazily in the chair in his office and looked around. I noticed the framed picture on the wall of the German submarine with men standing on top.

He noticed me looking. "My sub, my crew. We used to sink American ships." He sounded proud.

"Shelves first," he said on my second day, voice low and edged. "Labels out. No gaps."

"Yes, sir."

"Count the drawer twice."

"Yes, sir."

He watched me face bottles until the lines were ruler straight.

He watched me mop until the bucket water ran clear.

He watched everything.

His wife trained me with a patience that felt like shade on a hot day. "Order book lives here," she said, tapping the counter. "Case counts here. Rotate stock. New to the back." She showed me how to angle bottles so the glass caught the light, how to spot a fake ID without making a scene, how to open a stubborn crate without splintering half the store.

I liked Bill and his wife. His rules were simple. You work hard; you get paid. Do your job well. Be competent.

He took me into his back office a few times after the store closed and told me stories of the war. He was proud of his service. He broke down on one occasions, barely controlling the tears, as he described how he had to surface his submarine to shoot American sailors, over 50 of them.

"It was war," he said, his voice choking. "That's the one thing I did that I regret. Those sailors didn't deserve that. But if they had been rescued, they could have continued fighting and we didn't have the room to take them as prisoners."

That was his human side. But the look on his face when a Jew came into the store…terrifying. He barely controlled his anger and hatred.

I guess some things never change.

The work narrowed my mind to one task at a time. Box in, box out. Face, front, align. The rhythm steadied me. I outlasted everyone. Months later, Bill nodded toward the time clock. "You've broke a record," he said, almost approving. "You've worked here far longer than anyone else. Most people do not have any discipline."

People asked how a seventeen-year-old could work in a liquor store. The bottles were sealed. That made it legal. I carded when I had to. I stocked. I counted. I learned the weight of a case of whiskey in my hands.

Behind the store, the village breathed in quarters. The penny arcade hummed with pinball bells, the clack of flippers, the tin music of machines that never slept. Dust hung in the light like a second skin.

After shifts, I fed coins to the slots and watched the silver ball rocket and ricochet, lights stuttering in tight bursts. The coins went fast. The noise calmed me and gave me a single task.

I worked hard because I wanted a car. This was a critical piece of the plan forming in my mind. A car meant a way off the mountain and out of that house.

In the meantime, Dad drove me to my job every day, then picked me up at night. Rain or shine, good weather or blizzard. That was his part of the deal.

That lasted for six months until the day it snowed. Hard. A huge snowfall that went on for hours and hours. But it was my job and my chance at getting a car.

Dad refused to drive me. Too dangerous he said. He was tired. He'd worked hard all day. I wouldn't understand hard work.

Bill called, "Where are you."

"Dad won't drive me," I stammered.

'Be here in two hours or find a new job." He hung up.

I walked five miles in one of the worst snowstorms I'd ever seen down to the liquor store and arrived just in time.

Bill nodded as I entered. "Good. Start sweeping."

A few hours later, with the only customer being the regular who purchased exactly one-half pint of 151 proof Bacardi rum every night, he drove me home.

Bill had some words for my dad.

"You let your son walk five miles in this weather," he said. "You should be ashamed of yourself."

"What?" My dad was furious. I thought they were going to come to blows. "How dare you…"

"Shut up," I'd never heard someone talk to my dad like this before. "For once in your life, listen."

"I'm listening."

"Your son could have died due to your negligence."

"Gotcha. Anything else?"

"No."

He turned and left. Dad just stared at the space where he had been for a few minutes, then said, "When the storm passes, you are buying a car."

Bill stood up for me. Wow. An adult had stood up for me, respected me enough to face Dad and say his mind. I was flabbergasted.

I slid into a brand new Toyota with my father as cosigner. The seats smelled of new vinyl and glue. The engine ticked after I turned it off, like a small animal settled under the hood. I learned distances the hard way, misjudged corners and bad angles in tight lots. One dent. Then another. By the time I let that car go, all four corners told on me.

That night, after closing, I locked the door, felt the latch catch, and stood for a second in the quiet. My hands smelled like cardboard, cleaner, and a hint of bourbon I never tasted. Mountain air came in cold. The parking lot lights buzzed. I put the keys in my pocket and headed for the arcade or home, one step closer to leaving.

The Gallery Shifts

The Blue Jay Gallery changed while I worked. At first it smelled like linseed oil and fresh canvas, my father's world. Paintings on the wall. We got some money when a piece sold. Clean.

Then, boxes started arriving with my mother's neat handwriting on the labels. Racks of cards. Shelves of mugs with bears and pines stamped in glaze. Jars of flavored coffee that made the place smell like hazelnut and vanilla.

"Tourists love to touch things," Mom said, arranging a display so the mugs made a tidy arc. "They want to take a piece of the mountain home."

Dad did not look up from his easel. "They can take a painting."

"Not everyone buys a painting, Jerry." She held up a bag of beans. "They will buy this."

I watched her carry cartons to the back. Inventory meant numbers first, hope later. We counted, mugs by the dozen, cards by the case. The register drawer opened and closed, paper receipts whispering. Money went out first and maybe came back later, if it came back at all.

A week later, the front room felt tighter. Card spinners clicked when people brushed past. Coffee pressed over the oil paint, sweet on the tongue. My father's canvases shared wall space with a lattice of shelves.

He finally set his brush down. "This is not a gift shop," he said, not loud, each word set where it could not be moved.

Mom kept her smile. "It is a gallery that makes money between paintings."

He pinched the bridge of his nose. "A gallery does not carry inventory. I paint. We sell. Simple."

"Simple does not pay rent in February," she said, tapping price tags straight.

Different day, same argument. Sometimes it got heated. Occasionally, I thought they were going to come to blows, but as far as I know they never had a physical altercation.

Tourists came in with cold cheeks and wind in their coats. They paused at the paintings, then drifted toward the coffee jars.

"Oh, smell this," a woman said, popping a lid she should not. "Mocha almond."

Mom glided over, gentle and firm. "Let me help you with that." She made small sales feel like small wins, two cards, a mug, a quarter pound of beans. The bell on the door rang steadily. The till filled slower.

In the back, my father worked a canvas of a hawk.

A man pointed at it. "Do you do people? Or dogs? My wife wants our lab over the fireplace."

Dad did not hesitate. "Wildlife only."

The man waited, as if the rest of the sentence might change. It did not. "…Shame," he said, and left his phone number anyway.

After he walked out, Mom set a hand on the counter. "Commissions pay well," she said, soft, not nagging. "The pet portraits you did were good, Jerry."

He grumbled without words, eyes on the hawk. "Not what I do."

Which led to more arguing.

I had seen the numbers on the days he said yes. Pet portraits moved fast and paid clean. He held the line, and the line held him.

By spring, the gallery sounded different. The metal card rack clicked in a rhythm I knew by heart. Mugs chimed when someone bumped a shelf. The register tape curled in white loops like shed skin. Paintings still sold, but you had to find them between displays. Some days the tourist stuff worked. Some days it sat and stared back at us, price tags gathering dust.

At closing, the coffee smell lingered long after the bell. I turned out the lights, and the easel's shadow leaned over a field of small things. Money used to come in clean. Now it left first and maybe came back. Even when it did, the room felt more crowded. Boxes, compromise, a kind of success that came one mug at a time.

The Village Levels

After a year and a half or two, Bill said the store would close. Investors wanted the village torn down and rebuilt as a mall. New was the sales pitch. Modern. Easy parking. The same sinking I felt when the pool table turned into a shelf settled in my gut. No one asked what I thought.

I left the liquor store and became the dairy manager at the only market in Lake Arrowhead. A big store with long aisles and a waxy floor that squeaked under shoes. My manager showed me the ropes and then let go of the rope.

"Use last year's numbers," he said, tapping the order sheets. "Add ten percent. Maybe twenty in December."

I did that. Ten percent for growth. Ten more for safety. Better extra than empty shelves.

Then storms closed the mountain for weeks. Trucks chained up and ground their way in. Tourists stayed home. Milk dated out. Cottage cheese turned. I stacked cases on dollies and hauled them out back. The owner watched me pass the office glass again and again, arms folded. I kept moving. I was not fired. Some mistakes are not yours. Some verdicts, too.

A young woman worked in the cheese department. Her name was Gretchen. She tended her case carefully, then ordered too little and ran out too often. I liked her and thought about asking her out. I never did. One afternoon her station stood empty and the case sat half full. My manager said, "Had to let her go."

The words landed like a cold coin. I did not argue. I stocked my case and watched how quickly a person can vanish from a place that needs them.

The beginning of the end came the week she forgot to order cheese entirely. Mike discovered the oversight on delivery day when the truck arrived with everything except her department's allocation. His face went through several shades of red before settling on purple.

"You're taking the pickup to Los Angeles," he told her, his voice tight with controlled fury. "Get down to the distributor and collect what we need. Richard's going with you to help load."

The three-hour drive south was a masterclass in uncomfortable silence. Gretchen gripped the steering wheel like she was strangling it, her jaw clenched so tight I could see the muscles working. Every mile marker we passed seemed to wind her fury tighter. I tried small talk once, maybe twice, then gave up and watched the landscape roll by. The return trip was worse…boxes of cheese filling the truck bed while the tension in the cab grew thick enough to cut. She was pissed the whole way there and back, and I couldn't blame her. Mike had turned her mistake into a public humiliation disguised as problem-solving.

Two weeks later, her station stood empty for good.

The Teachers Who Opened Doors

Mr. Nicholas, History

Mr. Nicholas was perhaps my favorite teacher of all. He understood something fundamental about motivation that most educators missed completely…you had to make students want to learn before you could teach them anything meaningful. He possessed an almost magical ability to transform dull subjects into compelling experiences, and somehow, we all had genuine fun while absorbing more information than we realized.

He taught several classes during my high school years, and I enrolled in every single one. For once, I paid attention, sitting up straight, even developing genuine respect for a teacher…something I could only say about two or three educators in my entire high school and college years.

One lecture remains vivid in my memory decades later. He was covering the Egyptian pyramids, distributing handouts filled with photographs and architectural drawings. He began speaking almost in a whisper, forcing the entire classroom to fall silent just to hear him. We had to strain to catch every word, creating an atmosphere of focused attention I'd rarely experienced in school.

Then suddenly, he exploded. Yelling, flailing his arms, jumping onto desks, standing on chairs…pure theatrical acrobatics designed to drive home whatever point he was making about ancient engineering or Pharaonic power. The dramatic contrast between the whispered introduction and the explosive climax certainly livened up what could have been another tedious afternoon of note-taking.

But Mr. Nicholas's real genius revealed itself when he introduced board war games to our curriculum. One day he produced a box containing "Pre-Stages Masterpack" - five separate games simulating different battles from the ancient world. Greek campaigns, Roman conquests, Egyptian warfare, each one designed to recreate historical conflicts through strategic gameplay.

We spent the entire semester playing those games. Initially, none of us understood what he was trying to accomplish through this apparent departure from traditional teaching methods. After a few weeks of learning rules and loosening up, we began having genuine fun while unconsciously absorbing lessons about ancient civilizations. Mr. Nicholas used those games to explain concepts of warfare, politics, economics, and diplomacy that would have been abstract and forgettable in lecture format.

We also played Risk and a game called Nuclear Destruction that perfectly captured Cold War anxieties. In Nuclear Destruction, each student controlled a different country equipped with factories for building either missiles or anti-missile systems. You could fire weapons at other nations or defend against incoming attacks. Alliances formed and dissolved based on strategic necessity, with all communication restricted to brief written messages passed between players.

We managed two or three complete games of Nuclear Destruction each semester. The experience was engaging. Mr. Nicholas skillfully used our investment in the outcomes to teach lessons about modern politics, international relations, and the delicate balance of nuclear deterrence.

I usually won those Nuclear Destruction games, which apparently impressed my classmates enough that some drew pictures parodying my strategic abilities. The combination of academic success and peer recognition in the same classroom was unprecedented in my high school experience.

Mr. Nicholas had discovered something profound: learning happens naturally when students are genuinely engaged, and engagement comes from making education feel like adventure rather than obligation.

Mr. Moore, English

One of my favorite teachers was Mr. Moore, and he was exactly what education should be. He understood that literature could be a gateway to everything else…reading us stories about ancient gods and goddesses, spaceships navigating distant galaxies, epic battles, heroic quests, and characters facing impossible odds. He used storytelling to make English class feel like an adventure rather than academic drudgery.

His approach worked brilliantly. I left his classroom each day genuinely excited about learning more, a feeling so rare in high school that it almost seemed miraculous. This wasn't a class where students watched the clock or counted the days until the semester's end…we actually wanted to be there, wanted to engage with whatever story or concept he'd introduce next.

Mr. Moore taught multiple classes throughout my time at Rim of the World High, and I signed up for every single one: two mythology courses, three science fiction classes, and two traditional English courses. Each one felt like discovering a new continent.

The mythology classes ignited a fascination with ancient religions that has stayed with me my entire life. One course focused on Greek and Roman myths…the familiar stories of Zeus and Apollo, but presented with depth and context that revealed their psychological and cultural significance. The other explored mythologies from around the world: Native American creation stories, Hindu epics, African folklore. Each tradition offered unique insights into how humans had always tried to make sense of existence, love, death, and meaning.

His English classes took a more traditional approach, focusing on writing mechanics, sentence structure, and the subtle complexities of grammar. Fortunately, I'd always loved the written language, so learning the technical foundations felt like understanding the engineering behind something I already appreciated. Mr. Moore made grammar feel like craftsmanship rather than arbitrary rules.

The science fiction class was an unexpected gift. I never imagined finding speculative fiction on a high school curriculum and immediately enrolled when I spotted it on the schedule. Even though I'd already read most of the assigned stories during my exploration, Mr. Moore brought fresh perspectives that made familiar tales glow with new meaning. He helped us see how science fiction writers used futuristic settings to examine contemporary human problems, how imagination could be a tool for understanding reality rather than escaping from it.

Mr. Moore proved that the right teacher could transform any subject into something compelling. He didn't just cover the curriculum…he opened doors to lifelong interests and showed us that learning could be genuinely enjoyable rather than something we endured for grades.

Mr. Key, Geology

When I discovered my new high school offered a geology class, I was genuinely excited. This seemed like the perfect opportunity to restore my previous love of rocks and geology…the love that had died because of its relationship to my Dad. I imagined learning about tectonic forces, seeing dramatic photographs of volcanic eruptions, maybe even taking field trips to examine rock formations firsthand.

Mr. Key had something potentially remarkable in his classroom...a student carrying the embers of genuine passion for his subject, waiting for the right teacher to rekindle that flame. Here was a chance to help someone reconnect with a fascination that had been buried under family complications, to separate the pure joy of geological discovery from the painful associations that had silenced it.

From the first day, Mr. Key approached geology as a bureaucratic obligation rather than a window into the earth's magnificent processes. Where I hoped to rediscover wonder in volcanic eruptions, he presented them as curriculum requirements. The forces that had once amazed me...the slow creation of mountains, the patient formation of crystals...became just topics to cover before moving on to the next unit.

His teaching style was as lifeless as the specimens in his dusty display cases. He delivered lectures from his chair in barely audible tones, treating the incredible story of our planet's formation like he was reading insurance policies. Students strained to hear explanations that should have been delivered with the excitement they deserved.

I watched my fragile hope for geological reawakening slowly suffocate in that quiet classroom. The subject that might have provided a refuge from family trauma instead became another disappointment, another door that closed rather than opened. Mr. Key's methodical coverage of required material was accurate but utterly devoid of the passion that could have healed my broken connection to the earth sciences.

By semester's end, any chance of rekindling my love for geology had been thoroughly extinguished. The embers I'd brought to his classroom had been smothered by institutional indifference disguised as education. It would take twenty-five more years before I could approach rocks and minerals again, finally rediscovering that childhood wonder through my own exploration, unrelated to Dad, far from classrooms and teachers who couldn't recognize the difference between teaching facts and nurturing fascination.

Mr. Key had been handed a perfect opportunity for educational healing and somehow managed to make the wound deeper instead.

Mr. Schweighardt, Physics

His teaching method was unconventional, to put it diplomatically. Each class followed the same ritual: ten-minute quiz on previous material, ten minutes reviewing homework, five minutes assigning new homework, then forty minutes of passionate lectures about his personal worldview. Physics became the minor subject in a course that was really about Schweighardt's interpretation of how the universe operated on spiritual, political, and moral levels.

I developed an immediate love-hate relationship with him. His lectures were genuinely fascinating…he could make connections between scientific principles and larger philosophical questions that most teachers never attempted. I learned about faith, corporate corruption, government overreach, and the moral obligations of educated citizens. But I learned remarkably little about velocity, acceleration, or electromagnetic theory.

The academic demands were significant. Since he spent most class time on personal philosophy rather than physics instruction, we had to master the textbook material largely through homework assignments that were more extensive than typical science classes required. You either taught yourself physics or you failed his tests.

I kept wondering how he got away with essentially preaching during public school hours, but his religious discussions were so refreshing compared to the sterile secularism of other classes that I never considered complaining to the administration. He talked about ultimate questions that mattered rather than just preparing us for standardized tests.

His worldview lectures covered everything from the spiritual emptiness of materialism to the corrupting influence of unchecked capitalism. He'd connect thermodynamics to moral principles or use electromagnetic fields as metaphors for divine influence. Whether you agreed with his conclusions or not, he forced students to think about physics as part of a larger framework rather than just isolated formulas to memorize.

By semester's end, I couldn't solve complex physics problems any better than when I'd started. But I'd absorbed lessons about intellectual integrity, moral courage, and the connections between scientific understanding and spiritual awareness that stayed with me for decades. Schweighardt taught life philosophy disguised as physics, and the life philosophy proved more valuable than the academic credit.

Looking back, I realize he was doing something remarkable…treating teenage students like they could grapple with complex ideas about meaning and purpose rather than just future test-takers. Most teachers avoided controversial topics to protect their jobs. Schweighardt risked his career to share what he believed students needed to know about navigating the world as thinking, moral beings.

Whether that made him a brilliant teacher or a poor one probably depends on what you think education is supposed to accomplish.

Mr. Farrell, Ecology

Pine resin, wet soil, cold air thin enough to taste. Mr. Farrell took class outside whenever he could. "Field notes, not essays," he said, handing out Rite in the Rain pads that felt official in the palm. "What you can count, you can protect."

We stood by the runoff ditch after a storm and watched silt cloud the water. "Upstream choices, downstream consequences," he said. "It's all connected." He had us trace a single candy wrapper from trail to culvert to lake. "Nothing disappears. It only moves."

On a quiet morning, he stopped us mid-hike. "Listen." The forest hummed so softly I felt my shoulders drop. He linked care to observation and made me believe looking closely was a way to serve.

Mr. Farrell made sense. He must have been good…I kept signing up for his classes year after year. Advanced biology, ecology, environmental science. Each one felt like an escape from the educational wasteland that surrounded his classroom.

I think I puzzled him, though. He could see I was smart…when I engaged, my reports were excellent. But I was losing interest in school rapidly. I couldn't keep my attention on anything. The whole educational system felt like a waste of time designed by people who'd never met an actual student.

Farrell knew I had potential. He'd catch me after class sometimes, trying to figure out why I wasn't applying myself consistently. I couldn't explain that his class was the only one that felt real, that everywhere else felt like performance theater with no connection to anything that mattered.

I tested him with a brief experiment. For our ecology report assignment, I'd recently read a fascinating article about dinosaur extinction theories. Instead of writing my own analysis, I copied the article word for word from the book and submitted it as my work.

Farrell loved it. Gave me an A+ and praised the sophisticated thinking. To make matters worse, I accidentally lent him the book a few weeks later. He never mentioned recognizing the text, so I assume he never got around to reading that chapter.

The following semester, Farrell was gone. The rumor mill said he'd gotten tired of trying to teach students who refused to learn. Last anyone heard, he'd fled to Guam where he was happily teaching kids who wanted to be there.

I felt guilty about the plagiarized report for years. Not because I'd cheated…the system was broken anyway. But because I'd wasted the one teacher who cared enough to try something different.

Mr. Exline, Biology

Mr. Exline and I had fundamentally different philosophies about education. Coming off Mr. Farrell's dynamic ecology class the previous semester, I'd developed genuine interest in biological science. Maybe even career-level interest. So I signed up for Exline's advanced biology course expecting more of the same engaging approach.

The classroom told me everything I needed to know. Where Farrell's walls displayed colorful ecosystem posters and shelves held live specimens, Exline's room was sterile as a morgue. No visual aids, no living examples, no props of any kind. Just bare walls, fluorescent lights, and rows of desks facing a blackboard. His approach was pure lecture and textbook memorization - exactly the kind of educational theater I'd grown to despise.

For the first month, we sat through PowerPoint presentations about cellular structures and listened to him read from the textbook. I watched my enthusiasm for biology drain away like water through a sieve. This wasn't science; this was data transfer disguised as learning.

Then Exline decided we needed some "hands-on experience."

He wheeled in a cart loaded with dead frogs floating in formaldehyde solution. The chemical smell hit the room like a toxic cloud, sharp and medicinal and completely revolting.

He placed one gray, lifeless carcass on each desk, then distributed scalpels and dissection kits with the casual efficiency of someone handing out pencils.

"Today we'll explore internal anatomy through direct observation," he announced, beginning his lecture on proper cutting techniques.

I stared at the dead frog on my desk. As a kid, I'd spent countless hours watching live frogs in ponds and streams. They were quick, clever, alive in ways that fascinated me. This pickled specimen was the opposite of everything that had made me love biology in the first place.

I leaned back, folded my arms across my chest, and fixed my gaze on the blackboard. When Exline told everyone to pick up their scalpels, I didn't move.

He ignored me for several minutes, probably hoping I'd eventually comply. When it became obvious I had no intention of cutting into that frog, he walked over to my desk.

"Is there a problem, Richard?"

I tried to explain. This wasn't learning - this was just following instructions to destroy something that had once been alive. If he wanted us to understand frog anatomy, there were diagrams, models, even videos that could show us internal structures without requiring us to hack apart corpses. The formaldehyde smell was making me nauseous, and the whole exercise felt pointless and cruel.

Exline listened with the patience of someone who'd dealt with difficult students before. He tried gentle persuasion first, then appeals to academic requirements, then subtle pressure about my grade. But I think he eventually recognized the particular brand of stubbornness that runs in my family. Lowes don't bend on principles, even inconvenient ones.

"Fine," he said finally. "But you still need to write the lab report."

I researched frog anatomy thoroughly and wrote a detailed analysis of every internal organ, complete with accurate descriptions of what I would have observed during dissection. The report was comprehensive, scientifically accurate, and demonstrated complete understanding of the material.

Exline gave me an A+. Whether he forgot I hadn't actually dissected anything or simply appreciated the quality of my research, the subject never came up again. By mutual agreement, we established that I wouldn't be cutting up any more dead animals, and he wouldn't penalize me for it.

The incident crystallized something important: there were multiple ways to learn the same information, and the most common approach wasn't always the most effective. Sometimes refusing to follow standard procedures opened up better alternatives that served everyone involved.

Mrs. Herlitz, Art

Mrs. Herlitz operated from a rigid aesthetic theology that divided the world into art and not-art, with herself as the sole arbiter of the distinction. Her doctrine was simple: abstract good, representation bad. The more literal an image, the more she dismissed it as mere "pigment on paper"…her favorite phrase for anything that dared to depict recognizable objects.

Initially, we coexisted peacefully. I attended her lectures, watched her show techniques, and completed assignments without enthusiasm or conflict. She struck me as dogmatic but harmless, just another teacher pushing a particular agenda I could ignore while collecting my grade.

She'd introduced us to linoleum carving, demonstrating the tools and techniques with obvious enthusiasm. Most students played it safe with small, simple designs…abstract shapes or basic patterns that fit comfortably on four-by-five-inch blocks.

I had bigger ambitions. I'd just finished reading *The Book of Skaith* and wanted to carve one of the memorable images from the story…a "Johnny Hangman Tree" with its distinctive twisted branches and ominous presence. I worked for a week on a nine-by-twelve-inch piece, carefully planning each cut, building layers of detail that brought the fictional tree to life in linoleum relief.

The finished carving was ambitious, technically accomplished, and dramatically more complex than anything else produced in class. I was genuinely proud of the work…it captured both the literary inspiration and showed mastery of the medium.

Mrs. Herlitz hated it.

Years later, I realized she'd taught me something valuable after all…how to recognize when someone's expertise was really just personal bias with institutional authority behind it. That lesson would prove useful in many contexts where supposed experts turned out to be ideological gatekeepers protecting their own limited worldview.

Mr. Chrissinger, Driver's Education

Mr. Chrissinger taught Driver's Education. We spent our classroom hours learning traffic laws, basic car mechanics, and listening to his detailed reports about the best parking spots for teenage romance around town…information that seemed more personally researched than professionally relevant.

The graduation requirement included three hours of actual driving time, divided across three weekends with three students per car. Each student got one hour behind the wheel while the other two provided commentary from the backseat. Mr. Chrissinger always drove with the boys while female teachers handled the girls' sessions.

Those sessions were educational torture. I'd never driven before…Dad wouldn't let me near our only car since the family's livelihood depended on its continued functionality. So, my first time behind a steering wheel happened with an audience of critics eager to document every mistake.

The mistakes were abundant and immediate. I forgot to signal turns, confused the gas and brake pedals, and generally operated the vehicle like someone who'd learned to drive by reading about it in a foreign language. Every error became ammunition for my backseat tormentors, who provided running commentary from the moment I got in until they dropped me off at home.

One bully fixated on a small wart on my upper lip, spending the entire first session describing how disgusting it looked and how it made him physically ill. His attention to this minor facial imperfection was so relentless that I went home and cut the thing off with a razor blade rather than endure another weekend of commentary. The next session, he simply found new material to work with.

The gas station incident provided weeks of entertainment for them. When Chrissinger told me to fill the tank, I'd never operated a gas pump before. I grabbed the first hose I saw and tried to force the nozzle into the car's intake. When it wouldn't fit, I kept trying until it sort of worked, then began pumping.

After about a dollar's worth of fuel, Chrissinger noticed I was putting leaded gas into an unleaded car and screamed to stop. He finished the job himself while my passengers added this spectacular failure to their growing collection of Richard driving stories.

Getting pulled over for driving too slowly in the freeway's fast lane created another classic tale. The officer was understanding…he could see the student driver sign and just wanted to explain the importance of maintaining traffic speed. But my companions treated the incident as if I'd been arrested for armed robbery.

I did everything wrong that was possible to do wrong. Left turns from the right lane, right turns from the left lane, wrong signals, missed red lights, inappropriate speeds in both directions. I changed lanes in front of a semi-truck, terrifying everyone, including myself. When someone cut me off and nearly forced us onto the shoulder, I learned that defensive driving was more than a classroom concept. Parallel parking defeated me completely…I gave up and accepted failure rather than provide more entertainment.

By the end of the third weekend's end, I never wanted to see another automobile. The combination of performance anxiety, mechanical ignorance, and constant ridicule had turned what should have been exciting into pure misery.

But time heals driving trauma. Dad eventually let me practice with our car on brief trips, and within a couple of years I had my license and my own car. The bullies moved on to torment other victims.

Then came the sweetest coincidence of my high school career. Both tormentors enrolled in a class where I served as teacher's aide, responsible for grading tests, reviewing papers, and supervising when the instructor was away. They'd forgotten about our shared driving experiences, but I remembered every cruel comment, every moment of humiliation they'd inflicted.

Their semester became an education in consequences. Every test got the most rigorous grading possible, every paper received the harshest critique I could justify, every assignment faced maximum scrutiny. They earned barely passing grades through genuine suffering, working harder for C-minuses than they'd ever worked for anything in their academic lives.

Watching them struggle for grades that should have come easily was profoundly satisfying. They never connected their classroom difficulties to their driver's education behavior, but I made sure they understood that academic success required more effort than they'd previously invested.

Sometimes revenge really is a dish best served cold, with a side of barely passing grades.

Mr. Golding, Fencing

Physical education and I maintained a relationship of mutual hostility throughout high school. It wasn't that I disliked physical activity or games…I enjoyed both when they didn't involve public humiliation. The problem was the toxic combination of adolescent awkwardness and the pack of bullies who saw PE class as their personal hunting ground. Traditional sports like football, baseball, and soccer became associated with torment rather than competition, and I grew to despise the entire physical education program.

While putting together my junior year schedule, I noticed an unusual offering: a class simply called "fencing." Sword fighting. That sounded infinitely more interesting than another semester of dodging footballs thrown at my head by kids who thought my pain was entertainment. I signed up immediately.

I loved fencing from the very first day. Mr. Golding taught the class with a genuine passion for both the sport and the teaching process. He enjoyed fencing himself, and his enthusiasm was infectious rather than performed. We took an immediate liking to each other, which made attending his class a pleasure instead of an ordeal to endure.

My friend Dan enrolled in fencing as well, which transformed the experience into something genuinely fun. We spent the next year developing our skills together, both becoming quite proficient at this unusual sport, though neither of us pursued the dedication required for true mastery.

Mr. Golding explained the three major types of fencing early in our training. Foil and epee both require hitting opponents with the sword's point only…foil restricts valid targets to the chest area, while epee allows hits anywhere on the body. Saber fencing permits only chest hits but accepts edge strikes rather than point contact. Each style demands different equipment and strategies.

The class focused primarily on foil fencing because of equipment limitations. We had about thirty foils…long, skinny swords with protective buttons at the tip. Only two sabers and one epee were available for the entire class. Foil also proved easiest to learn, making it the logical starting point for beginners.

Dan and I experimented with saber technique occasionally, though we never developed real competence. Saber fencing proved much more physically demanding and technically complex than either foil or epee.

Each class followed the same structure: ten minutes of warm-up exercises followed by forty minutes of actual fencing. Since we were scheduled for the last period of the day, showering wasn't required…students could clean up at home. This arrangement was necessary because fencing operated outside the physical education department's jurisdiction. We weren't allowed access to locker rooms or showers, and the PE coaches did not try to hide their disdain for our "inferior" sport.

I spent over a year in that class, gradually mastering foil technique and strategy.

For the first (and only) time in my teenage years, I genuinely enjoyed a sport.

For the first (and only) time, a physical education instructor treated me with respect and encouragement.

For the first time, I excelled in athletic competition.

The combination of individual skill development, strategic thinking, and a supportive environment created an experience that was both educational and genuinely enjoyable.

Fencing taught me that physical activity could be rewarding when separated from the social dynamics that made traditional PE classes unbearable.

What They Left Me

Mr. Nicholas left me decisions under pressure. Mr. Moore left me sentences you can hear breathe. Mr. Key left me patience with layers you can't see yet. Mr. Schweighardt left me predict, test, adjust. Mr. Exline left me patterns and the honest mess. Mr. Farrell left me attention as stewardship. Mrs. Herlitz left me the knowledge to start again when the page fights back. Mr. Chrissinger left me calm as a technique.

I didn't belong to many groups, but I belonged in these rooms. Each one gave me a way to think with my hands or my eyes or my voice, and that was enough to keep me moving forward with a little more trust in myself.

Breaking my Mom's Heart

Prom season hit like perfume in the halls. Glitter on flyers. Balloons taped to lockers. Girls comparing dresses by the bathroom mirrors, fabric swishing like rain. I kept my eyes on my books and my hands in my pockets.

At dinner, Mom tried a soft entry. "Prom's next week," she said, sliding a casserole to the center. "You'll have a great time."

"I'm not going," I said, steady.

Dad looked up from his plate. "You will go," he said. He turned back to his meal, subject closed.

"I don't have a girlfriend," I said. The fork felt heavy. The room smelled of baked cheese and oregano. "I'm not going."

He set his fork down. "I don't care. Your mom wants you to go, you will go."

The memory of the Christmas living room at my grandmother's house flashed through my head. Smelled the pine cleaner and tasted the turkey and ham glaze. With Dad's breath close to me, smelling strongly of coffee. His threat of telling everything, the naked photos, the mockery. The vow I made. I felt it lock in again.

Then a quick flashback of seeing myself in the mirror, just six years old, pressed to the bed by his body. I felt the same pain, the shame, and the disgust.

"I'm not going," I said, lower now.

His jaw worked once, then he went back to eating, the scrape of metal on ceramic louder than it needed to be. Mom tried to smile. It did not hold. No more words were said.

Later that night, I heard a soft sound from the living room. Mom was sitting on the couch, the room dark except for the glow of the streetlights through the window. Her shoulders shook. She was crying. I stood in the hallway, unseen. It was a dream of hers, I realized, a picture she'd held onto, and I had just broken it. The silence in the house felt heavier than any argument.

Apparently, I was responsible for Mom's happiness.

I held my ground and didn't go to the prom.

This was a hill I was fully willing to die on.

Giving in for Graduation

The week of graduation, the caps and gowns arrived at school. Cardboard boxes opened with a papery sigh. The fabric felt thin under my fingers. I left mine in the bag and pushed it to the back of my closet.

At breakfast, Dad noticed. "You are going to graduation," he said, voice like a door closing. "Like it or not."

"I do not want to get up on stage," I said. Toast cooled on my plate and butter went glossy and dull. "I just want the diploma. I don't need to be there to get that."

He leaned forward, eyes clear. "You are going," he said. No heat. No shout. Stone set on stone. "You finished. You will do as I say." He stood, carrying a plate to the sink. His hand dipped to the belt. "or would you rather…"

I looked at Mom. She folded her napkin and set it down. "It's just one day," she said. "Give me that."

I nodded once. "Fine." Better than continuing the argument and getting the belt. Better than being told I was property and would do as I was told like a good little piece of furniture.

Graduation day smelled like cut grass and sunscreen. The metal chairs out on the field baked in the sun. Programs flapped like small flags in people's hands. A PA speaker hissed, then cleared, and a principal's voice rolled out in formal phrases. My gown whispered at my shins when I walked. The cap sat wrong. The tassel tickled my temple.

I found my row and sat. Names started. Applause rose and fell like waves. Heat gathered under the robe. I listened for my name the way you listen for a kettle to click off.

"Richard," the announcer said, clear enough to cut through the haze.

I stood. The world narrowed to steps and a handshake. The principal's palm was dry and firm. The cardboard diploma case pressed flat and real against my fingers. Cameras clicked. A cheer went up from somewhere left of the fifty-yard line. I kept my eyes forward and kept moving.

On the grass beyond the stage, kids hugged and cried and threw caps. I walked to the edge of the chaos and breathed. The air tasted like summer. The mountain sat blue on the horizon. For a second I felt taller inside my skin.

My parents found me by the fence. Mom's eyes shone. She smoothed the sleeve of my gown with her fingertips, as if the fabric could store the moment. "Let me see you," she said, stepping back to frame me with her hands like a picture.

Dad gave a single nod that felt like a stamp. "Good," he said. "You did it." Then he had to add, "Just like I told you."

We took a photo near the bleachers. The metal left faint lines on my palm when I leaned against it. The tassel brushed my cheek. For the first time in a long time, the noise around me sounded like background, not threat.

Later, at home, I slipped the cap on my desk and opened the empty diploma case. The felt inside was smooth and dark. I thought about the field, the handshake, the click of cameras, the way my name sounded carried on a speaker over grass and sun. I had not wanted to go. He made me go. Sometimes it's just easier to give in.

But I swore this would be the last time. I was not property. I was more than a piece of furniture.

What I Took With Me

High school ended without fanfare in my head. I had a car and money that I earned. My job became the first part of my plan to get out of this hellhole.

What I didn't take with me was Belinda. She was still a few years from being able to leave, still in that house, still navigating the same rooms I'd spent nineteen years mapping. That cost something. I told myself she was older now, more capable, that Dad had gotten less physical as I got bigger and pushed back. I told myself she'd be fine. I needed to believe that to go.

She was fine. She's wonderful. But I think about the girl standing in the doorway watching me load boxes into a U-Haul, and I hope she knew what I couldn't say out loud: that she was the reason I'd stayed as long as I did, and that leaving wasn't the same as abandoning.

And it was about to get an order of magnitude worse.

Chapter 10: The Day I Almost Died

On Christmas day, after we'd finished unwrapping presents and the living room floor was littered with torn wrapping paper and ribbons, Mom looked at Dad with that expression that meant she had something on her mind.

"You two should go for a hike," she said, nodding toward me and then Dad. "Would be good for the two of you to bond. Spend some time together."

Dad's face showed exactly how he felt about that suggestion. He glanced up from his coffee with obvious reluctance, then at me, then back at Mom.

"I don't really want to…" I started, but Mom cut me off.

"It's Christmas. You're going. Both of you." Her tone left no room for argument.

Dad set down his cup with a slight grimace. It had been quite some time since he and I had done anything together that didn't involve carrying his art supplies, and neither of us seemed particularly enthusiastic about breaking that pattern.

"Come on," he said finally, resignation clear in his voice. "Let's get this over with."

"Where?" I asked.

He gestured toward the window. "Down a creek off Route 18. Good day for it."

The perfect hiking area was about two blocks from our house, across the main road on the mountain called Route 18. Just after the road, the mountain began its long drop into the San Bernardino valley in a beautiful series of cliffs and valleys. Our house was located near a bend in the road, which was caused by a small stream known as Strawberry Creek.

We started around 8 AM, stepping into air that was chilly but pleasant. The morning held that crisp freshness that promised a beautiful day ahead. It had snowed a few days before, leaving small patches of ice crystals sparkling in shadowy spots, but the sun was already warming the rocks and melting the frost from exposed surfaces. The sky was that perfect California blue that makes you understand why people move here. Not a cloud in sight, nothing to suggest the storm that would roll in later. It seemed like the ideal day for a casual hike.

We planned on a short, simple hike of perhaps two hours. Because of this, we both ate a simple breakfast consisting of toast and coffee for Dad, cereal for me, but didn't pack a lunch or any other accessories. We wanted to be back home well before lunch, so didn't see any reason to carry extra weight around for what should be a casual Christmas morning stroll.

"Won't need jackets," Dad said, testing the air temperature with his hand. "Feels like it'll warm up nice."

We started by crossing Route 18, waiting for a logging truck to rumble past, its diesel engine echoing off the mountain walls. The asphalt was still cold under our feet, but the sun felt warm on our backs as we stepped onto the rocky ground beyond the road's edge.

Dad pointed toward the creek bed. "Follow the water down. Easier than fighting through all that brush on the ridge."

The stream bed was indeed beautiful. Strawberry Creek had carved a winding path through granite and sandstone, creating pools and small waterfalls every few hundred yards. The sound of moving water provided a constant background music. Sometimes a gentle gurgle over smooth stones, sometimes a more dramatic splash where the creek dropped over rock ledges.

We walked in tense silence at first. Dad wasn't much of a talker under the best circumstances, and being forced into this father-son bonding experience had made him even more withdrawn. I could feel his resentment radiating like heat from a stove. Neither of us wanted to be here, and we both knew it.

But as we followed the creek deeper into the canyon, something began to shift. The crunch of our footsteps on loose gravel and fallen leaves, the whisper of wind through pine branches, the distant call of a hawk circling overhead. These sounds gradually eased the tension between us.

"Careful there," Dad said quietly when I reached toward some plants near the water's edge. "Looks like stinging nettle. Poison oak over there too."

His voice had lost some of its earlier edge. When a bright blue jay landed on a branch nearby, I caught him studying it with genuine interest, his artist's eye automatically cataloging the play of light on feathers.

"Look at that," he said, pointing to a spot where the morning sun hit a small waterfall, creating tiny rainbows in the mist.

I nodded, and for a moment we stood together watching the light show without the usual awkwardness that defined our interactions. Maybe this was his way of sharing something important with me, showing me how to really see the world instead of just looking at it.

We both gradually withdrew into ourselves, but it was a calmer withdrawal now, less defensive. The canyon was working its magic on us, stripping away the household tensions and allowing us to exist in the same space without conflict.

Down into the creek bed we went. We hiked for an hour, then another hour, then another. The stream gradually widened and deepened as smaller tributaries joined it from hidden canyons. What had started as a creek you could step across became a stream that required careful rock-hopping, then eventually a small river that gurgled and sang as it flowed around boulders the size of cars.

"Should probably head back," Dad said when we paused at a particularly scenic pool surrounded by massive granite walls.

But then we'd see another bend ahead, hear the distant sound of falling water, catch a glimpse of sunlight hitting rock faces we hadn't seen yet.

"Just a little further," I'd say.

"Yeah," Dad would agree. "Let's see what's around that corner."

The canyon was alive with sounds. The constant rush and chatter of moving water, the scrape of our boots on stone, the occasional crack of a branch settling in the warming air. Birds called to each other from invisible perches high in the pine trees that clung to the canyon walls. Every few hundred yards we'd disturb a lizard that would skitter across the rocks with a sound like tiny fingernails on glass.

After perhaps four or five hours of walking, the sound ahead of us changed. Instead of the familiar babble of water over stones, we heard something deeper, more powerful. A low rumble that grew louder as we approached.

"Waterfall," Dad said, stating the obvious but with satisfaction in his voice.

We rounded the final bend and stopped in our tracks. The stream leaped out into space where it met a two hundred foot cliff, forming a gorgeous waterfall that crashed into a pool far below. The air was filled with mist and the thunderous sound of thousands of gallons per minute hitting stone. Rainbows danced in the spray, appearing and disappearing as the mist shifted in the breeze.

"Well, I'll be damned," Dad said, which for him was practically poetry.

Naturally, we couldn't allow a little thing like a cliff to stop us. Dad studied the rock face like he was planning a military operation, his eyes following potential routes down.

"There," he said, pointing to a steep slope immediately to the right of the stream bed. "That shale looks stable enough."

The descent was treacherous. Loose rock shifted under our feet with every step, threatening to start a landslide that would carry us down faster than we wanted to go. I found myself moving from handhold to handhold, sometimes on all fours, testing each footstep before committing my full weight.

"Easy," Dad called when a small cascade of stones rattled down past us. "Take your time."

At the base was a wonderful pool of clear, cold water, maybe fifty feet across and perfectly circular. The waterfall thundered into one end while a gentle stream flowed out the other, continuing its journey toward the valley below. Steep canyon walls surrounded us on all sides, creating a natural amphitheater that felt completely cut off from the modern world. The only sounds were falling water and the echo of our voices off the stone walls.

"This is incredible," I said, my words bouncing back from multiple directions.

Dad nodded, already studying the light patterns on the water, the way shadows fell across the rock faces. "Never seen anything like it."

We sat on a boulder for several minutes, sharing the kind of comfortable silence that comes from witnessing something genuinely beautiful together. The air smelled of wet stone and pine, sharp and clean in a way that made you want to take deeper breaths.

But the adventure wasn't over. After exploring the pool area, we continued following the stream as it wound deeper into the canyon system. The walls grew higher, the vegetation thicker. Ancient pines and oak trees created a canopy that filtered the sunlight into shifting patterns of light and shadow.

We continued walking down the stream bed for perhaps another hour, each turn revealing new wonders. Smaller waterfalls, deep green pools, rock formations that looked like abstract sculptures. It was early afternoon when we finally turned back for home, both of us hungry and beginning to feel the effects of our extended exploration.

"Better head back," Dad said, checking his watch. "Mom'll be wondering where we got to."

The return journey started pleasantly enough. We retraced our steps along the stream, stopping occasionally to rest and admire views we'd missed on the way down. But after about thirty minutes of uphill hiking, Dad's pace began to slow.

"You okay?" I asked when he stopped to lean against a large boulder.

"Yeah, just…" He pressed his hand against his chest, his face suddenly pale. "Give me a minute."

That minute stretched into several. Dad's breathing became labored, and beads of sweat appeared on his forehead despite the cool air in the shaded canyon.

"Dad?"

"I think…" He sat down heavily on a fallen log. "I think I'm having a heart attack."

The words hit me like a physical blow. Heart attack. Out here, miles from any road, hours from any help. Dad looked gray, his skin taking on an ashen color that scared me more than anything I'd seen before.

"What should we do?" I asked, trying to keep the panic out of my voice.

Dad was quiet for a long moment, his hand still pressed against his chest, breathing carefully. When he looked up at me, his eyes held a seriousness I'd rarely seen.

"You need to go get help," he said finally. "I can't make it back up that cliff. Can't walk any further."

"I'm not leaving you here."

"You have to." His voice carried that tone of absolute authority I knew better than to argue with. "Go back to the house. Get the rangers. I'll wait here."

"But what if..."

"I'll be fine. Just go. Fast as you can."

I looked around at the steep canyon walls, the tumbled rocks, the sheer distance we'd have to cover to reach help. Dad was asking me to leave him alone in the wilderness while he was having a heart attack. Every instinct told me this was wrong, but I couldn't see any alternative.

"Okay," I said. "I'll come back with help."

"I know you will."

I started up the canyon, looking back every few steps until Dad disappeared around a bend. Then I was alone with the sound of my own footsteps and the distant murmur of the stream.

The climb back to the waterfall took about thirty minutes, each step feeling heavier than the last. When I reached the cliff face, the shale slope that had seemed manageable going down now looked like a nearly vertical wall of loose rock. Every step sent small avalanches rattling down into the pool below.

I climbed carefully, testing each handhold, trying not to think about what would happen if I fell. The rocks were sharp against my palms, and several times I had to stop when loose stone shifted under my weight. My legs burned from the effort, and my lungs worked hard in the thin mountain air.

After what felt like hours but was probably only thirty minutes, I finally hauled myself over the top of the cliff, gasping and covered in rock dust. But that was just the beginning. I still had to find my way back through the maze of canyons and ridges that separated me from home.

The stream bed continued upward, branching into two distinct canyons after another thirty minutes of hiking. I stood at the junction, completely uncertain which path would lead me home. Both looked equally promising and equally treacherous.

I chose the right fork, thinking it seemed like an easier climb and hoping both canyons would eventually reach the top of the mountain. The afternoon sun was already starting to sink toward the western peaks, and I was beginning to understand that I was racing against time and my own endurance.

After another hour of steady climbing, my heart sank. The canyon dead-ended in another cliff, this one offering no obvious route to the top. I stood at the base of the rock wall, feeling the first real stirrings of panic.

"Think," I told myself aloud, my voice echoing off the stone walls. "There has to be a way."

I decided to attempt the cliff climb, thinking I might make better time on top of the hills than struggling through the canyon bottom. The rock face was broken and weathered, offering plenty of handholds but also plenty of opportunities for fatal mistakes.

The climb was exhausting. My arms ached from pulling myself up, and my legs shook with fatigue as I searched for footholds. Several times I had to stop and rest, clinging to the rock face while I caught my breath and planned my next move.

When I finally reached the top, I discovered a new problem. The entire hilltop was covered with thick, thorny bushes that formed an impenetrable tangle. I tried to push through the maze of branches and thorns, but my progress was impossibly slow. Each step required fighting through vegetation that grabbed at my clothes and scratched my exposed skin.

After struggling for what felt like hours but was probably only twenty minutes, I realized it was hopeless. I would be lost in this thorny maze long before I made any meaningful progress toward home. My energy was already running low, and the temperature was starting to drop as the sun sank lower.

I worked my way back down the cliff, a terrifying descent that was somehow worse than going up, and returned to the canyon junction. This time I took the left fork, the path I should have chosen originally.

By now I was feeling the effects of the long day. My head pounded with what I assumed was hunger - we'd eaten only a light breakfast many hours ago. My body felt drained, as if someone had pulled a plug and let all my energy flow out. The temperature was definitely dropping as afternoon moved toward evening, and clouds were beginning to gather around the higher peaks.

To make things worse, it looked like it might rain.

I stumbled up the rocky stream bed, forcing one foot in front of the other through sheer willpower. Every step required conscious effort, and I found myself stopping to rest more and more frequently. The sound of my own labored breathing seemed unnaturally loud in the gathering dusk.

That's when I tripped.

My foot caught on a submerged rock, and I went down hard, splashing face-first into the icy stream. The shock of the cold water drove the air from my lungs, and for a moment I just lay there, too exhausted to pull myself up.

When I finally dragged my body over to a nearby fallen log, I was soaked, shivering, and completely spent. My breath came in ragged gasps, my strength was gone, and I was getting cold, very cold. The wet clothes clung to my skin, conducting away what little body heat I had left.

"To heck with it," I told myself, my voice barely a whisper. "I can't go any further. I'm gonna die out here in the middle of the wilderness."

The words hung in the air, and as soon as I said them, I felt something shift inside me. The fight went out of my body, and I laid back against the log, ready to accept whatever was coming. I really felt like I was going to die in that canyon, far from any help, with Dad still waiting for rescue that might never come.

The forest sounds seemed to grow louder in the gathering darkness. The rustle of small animals in the underbrush, the distant hoot of an owl, the whisper of wind through pine needles. Stars were beginning to appear between the clouds, and I found myself wondering if these would be the last things I'd ever see.

I must have fallen asleep, because suddenly I jerked awake with a start. Something had disturbed me - a sound, a movement, I wasn't sure what. I looked around but didn't see anything unusual. Just the same canyon walls, the same stream, the same fallen log that had become my resting place.

But something had changed inside me during that brief sleep. When I opened my eyes, God was there in front of me. Not a voice from everywhere and nowhere - a presence, right there, unmistakable and real. This was not my time, He told me. I had a full life ahead of me, things to accomplish, experiences I hadn't had yet. Besides, this would have been a damn silly way to go - dying of exhaustion in a canyon on Christmas day because I'd gotten lost trying to save my father.

The encounter filled me with calm certainty. I would survive this.

But along with that spiritual reassurance came a flood of very earthly anger. As I pulled myself up from the log and began walking forward again, my mind churned with resentment. Dad was the adult here. It was his job to check the weather forecast, to bring adequate supplies, to plan a route he could actually handle. He'd failed at every single responsibility a father should have in this situation, and now I was the one paying the price for his incompetence.

This wasn't leadership or protection. This was just another example of his dangerous inability to think beyond his immediate impulses. He'd dragged me into a life-threatening situation through pure carelessness, then expected me to save both of us when his poor planning predictably fell apart.

It took every bit of willpower I possessed, but I forced one leg to move, then the other. Slowly I began making progress up the canyon, toward home and help. Each step was a conscious decision, a small victory over the part of me that wanted to give up.

It slowly began to get dark as night fell over the mountains. The snow was falling harder now, fat flakes that stuck to my wet clothes and melted against my skin, making me even colder. I barely noticed the increasing intensity of the storm. Every bit of my attention was focused on the simple act of moving forward. I blanked my mind to everything except walking, concentrating only on the next step, then the next one after that.

The hours passed in a blur of exhaustion, determination, and growing cold. The snow was accumulating on the ground now, making the rocks slippery and harder to navigate in the darkness. My feet found their own rhythm on the increasingly treacherous terrain, and I entered an almost meditative state where nothing existed except the need to keep moving. Step after step after step, always upward, always toward home, even as the winter storm intensified around me.

Then, cutting through the sound of wind, falling snow, and my own labored breathing, I heard something that made me stop dead in my tracks.

"Richard!"

I stood perfectly still, listening. Was I hallucinating? The voice seemed to come from somewhere ahead of me, but it was so faint I couldn't be sure I'd really heard it.

A few minutes later, the call came again, slightly louder this time.

"Richard! Are you out there?"

Wait a minute. That sounded like Belinda's voice.

I began running toward the sound, my exhausted body somehow finding new energy. The voice grew louder and clearer as I stumbled uphill, calling back as loudly as my hoarse throat would allow.

"Help!" I managed to croak. "Help! Help! Help!"

Finally, through the darkness and falling snow, I saw them. Three figures standing on what looked like a dirt path just below the main road. Belinda, Mom, and a man I slowly recognized as Curt Brey, one of my parents' friends. Snow was accumulating on their shoulders and hats, and they were all bundled up against the cold.

I collapsed on the path, gasping for air while they gathered around me.

"Dad's down there," I said between breaths, pointing back down the canyon. "He's had a heart attack or something. He sent me to get help."

Curt didn't wait to hear any more details. He took off immediately, running down the canyon with the confident stride of someone who knew these mountains well. Within moments he had disappeared into the darkness.

"You made it," Mom said, her voice thick with relief and worry. "We've been looking for you for hours."

Curt was a forest ranger, and he'd come to help in response to Mom's call for assistance. Since we were supposed to be home before lunch, she'd naturally become very worried as the day wore on. When we still hadn't returned by late afternoon, she was convinced something was wrong and called the forest service for help.

Curt's partner helped me over to his truck, where the heater was running and the cab was warm and dry. When I told him I was extremely hungry, he opened some K-rations and let me eat while we waited for news from Curt.

The food tasted better than anything I'd ever eaten. Simple military rations became a feast when you'd been running on empty for hours. We sat there in the warm truck, eating and listening to the radio, while Curt's voice crackled over the walkie-talkie every few minutes with progress reports.

"Still heading down the canyon."

"Found the waterfall."

"No sign of him yet."

Finally, at about 8:00 in the evening, Curt's voice came over the radio with the news we'd been waiting for.

"Found him. He's okay, just cold and tired. Built himself a shelter."

It turned out Dad had used his survival training from the Air Force. When it became clear he'd be spending the night in the canyon, he'd dug himself a burrow in a sheltered spot and covered his body with leaves and pine needles to stay warm and dry. The rangers found him buried in his improvised shelter, uncomfortable but unharmed.

The next day, a helicopter flew down into the canyon, braving high winds and tricky downdrafts to hoist Dad out of the wilderness. As a memorial to the rescue, the rangers named the landing spot "Lowe's Meadow."

Dad turned out to be fine. He hadn't had a heart attack after all. He'd suffered what doctors called a hypoglycemic attack, caused by low blood sugar from not eating enough that day. He recovered completely as soon as he got some food in him.

But I never forgot that day, and what I learned about my father's judgment. The day I almost died in the wilderness because of his failure to plan or prepare, saved only by my own perseverance and what felt like divine intervention. The day I learned that I was stronger than I thought, that I could push through exhaustion and fear when everything depended on it, but also that my father was fundamentally unreliable in crisis situations.

This experience crystallized something that had been building for years: my determination to get away from him as soon as possible. He wasn't just emotionally distant or occasionally cruel. He was actually dangerous. His poor judgment, his tendency toward melodrama, his complete failure to take responsibility for basic safety. These weren't just character flaws, they were genuine threats to my survival.

I never doubted my own strength quite the same way again. But I also never again trusted my father to keep me safe.

Chapter 11: In Between

The Scholarship Myth

Time for college. I tried to find a scholarship, diving into application after application believing merit would matter. All that crap people spout nowadays about white privilege? It's not true. I got rejected from dozens of scholarships because I was a white kid. Simple as that.

No one said that out loud, but it was true. The scholarships all went to minorities. I was just as qualified as anyone else, just as deserving, but I couldn't get a scholarship to save my life.

Don't talk to me about white privilege. It's bullshit.

The rejection letters piled up like autumn leaves, each one reminding me the system wasn't designed for kids like me. Kids whose parents had businesses but wouldn't help. Kids who were technically middle-class but functionally broke when it came to college expenses.

"Did you hear back from any scholarships?" Mom asked one evening, not looking up from inventory sheets spread across the kitchen table.

"All rejections."

"Well, you'll figure something out. We can't help you, you know. The gallery needs every penny."

"I know." I'd stopped expecting help years ago.

Dad looked up from his coffee. "Maybe if you'd help us in the store, we could..."

"I'm not working for free."

"You're living here for free," he shot back.

"Because I'm your son. Not your slave."

The conversation ended there, as most of our conversations did. With silence and the rustle of business papers.

Summer Prison

I spent the summer at home, which was its own kind of torture. I refused to help my parents in their gallery, period. They weren't going to pay me, and I don't work for free. Bad enough being stuck in the house with them. I couldn't imagine spending even more time with them in the store. That would have been worse than torture, especially because all they did was argue. At least when I was home and they were both working, I had some peace from the constant screaming and yelling.

"The tourist season's starting," Dad announced one morning. "We need extra help."

"Richard could help," Mom suggested, like I wasn't sitting right there.

"I have a job. At the supermarket. Where they actually pay me."

"Family business comes first," Dad said.

"Then pay me like family business. Minimum wage, at least."

"You don't pay family," Dad said, his voice taking on that edge I knew too well.

"Then I'm not working there."

I could see the vein in his temple start to throb. "You're living under my roof..."

"And I'm paying for my own car, my own gas, my own everything else." I stood up from the breakfast table. "The supermarket needs me in an hour."

I walked out before he could respond. The argument would continue without me, as most of their arguments did.

The area was beautiful, I'll give it that. At that time, Lake Arrowhead wasn't overbuilt like it is now. I spent time exploring, hiking in the woods, chilling out. There wasn't much else to do. I continued working at the supermarket. I had to keep that money flowing for car payments. I wasn't making enough for my own place.

The mountains offered the only refuge from family madness. Walking through pine forests where the only sounds were wind through branches and my own footsteps, I could pretend for a few hours that I lived in a different world. A world where parents didn't turn every conversation into warfare, where home meant safety instead of strategic navigation.

The Depression Economics

I got mixed messages from Dad about women. On one hand, Mom was on a pedestal. The highest pedestal of all. She was almost a goddess and he almost worshipped her. Despite the constant fighting and arguing, despite the constant open warfare between them, in his eyes, no one else compared to her. It wouldn't have surprised me to see him giving her offerings... well, perhaps he did. She received a constant stream of antiques, furniture, gifts, whatever else he thought she needed to pull her out of depression.

That was a constant throughout my entire early life: Mom's depression. She mostly kept it hidden from us children, but it was obvious. She'd get super depressed, and Dad would buy her something to bring her out of it. I learned some very bad lessons about money from this. You get depressed, you buy something. That's how you get out of depression.

I watched this pattern play out one week when Mom barely got out of bed for three days straight.

"She's not feeling well," Dad explained, which was his code for depression.

"Is she sick?"

"Sort of." He was already reaching for his car keys. "I'm going to town. Need to pick up something for the store."

But when he came back, it wasn't with store inventory. It was with an antique rocking chair that cost more than I made in two months at the supermarket.

"Look what I found for you, honey," he said, wheeling it into the living room like he'd discovered buried treasure.

Mom's face lit up for the first time all week. "Oh, Jerry, it's beautiful."

"I thought you'd like it. The dealer said it's from the 1890s."

And just like that, her depression lifted. For a while.

This pattern created a house where emotions were currency and objects were band-aids. Every antique chair, every piece of jewelry, every "surprise" was really Dad's desperate attempt to fix something that couldn't be purchased. But I was absorbing it all, learning that love meant spending money, that problems could be solved with the right acquisition, that feelings were just another transaction waiting to happen.

Whispers and Fractures

I got this rumor, unsubstantiated, that my mom had had an affair with a fireman. Just whispers I overheard during arguments. The pattern of their heated discussions changed, became more vehement. I got the distinct impression that the air between them had turned frosty, and it was because Mom went outside the marriage. But Dad seemed to shrug that off for the most part. As if he simply didn't believe it, didn't accept it, or didn't care. I have no idea because no one talked to me about it.

I first caught wind of it during one of their late-night arguments. I was in my room, trying to read, when their voices escalated beyond the usual volume.

"...can't believe you're bringing this up again," Mom was saying.

"Well, maybe if you hadn't..." Dad's voice dropped, but I caught the word "fireman."

"That was nothing, Jerry. How many times do I have to tell you?"

"Nothing? You call spending every afternoon..."

"Stop it. Just stop it."

The argument continued, but they'd lowered their voices. I pressed my ear to the floor, trying to catch more, but could only make out fragments. Something about volunteer work at the fire station. Something about "more than work." Something about "everyone's talking."

The not-knowing was worse than knowing would have been. Adult secrets hung in the air like smoke, visible but untouchable. I could sense the shifted dynamics, the new edges to their fights, the way certain words would make them both go silent. But I was locked out of understanding, left to piece together fragments of overheard conversations and meaningful glances.

The Sacred and the Damned

When I was young, we'd been members of the Church of Christ, a very strict religious sect. One of the things they preach is that sex is evil outside of marriage, and that's not all that great inside marriage either. Looking at a person of the opposite sex will get you struck down into hell faster than you can sing a lullaby. That's how I grew up. You don't look at women. You don't talk to them. You treat them with respect, but you hold them at a distance.

Looking back now, from my vantage point at 65, I'll tell you, I was one confused teenager. On one hand, my upbringing said women were sacred, God's gift to man. On the other, they were the ultimate source of evil because even looking at them would get you struck down to hell. Literally that black and white.

That combined with the constant teasing from my father (that never stopped, by the way), can you blame me for not wanting to go to the prom? For never having a girlfriend until long after college? My entire upbringing and the environment around me told me conflicting things about women, but the most important thing was that I really didn't want to go to hell. It didn't seem like a good alternative at all.

"You ever going to ask a girl out?" Dad would needle me during dinner.

"I don't know," I'd mumble.

"What's wrong with you? When I was your age..."

"When you were my age, you weren't being told that looking at girls was a sin," I shot back.

"That church stuff is just... guidelines," he said dismissively.

"Guidelines that lead to eternal damnation."

"You're too literal, son."

But how else was I supposed to take it? The same people who taught me that lying was wrong and stealing was wrong also taught me that desire was wrong. It all seemed equally serious to my teenage brain.

The Isolation Deepens

I was stuck at home for the most part. I didn't have any friends. In San Bernardino, the homes were relatively close together, so it was easy to form friendships. Those were kids from school, and most lived within short walking distance of our house. But in Lake Arrowhead, there was a long distance between every person. It didn't create an environment for making friends, and I was feeling so introverted and miserable that I wouldn't have been a great friend anyway.

Belinda and I had each other. That sounds like a small thing but it wasn't. The mountain had stripped away everything else — the neighborhood kids, the walkable streets, the easy proximity of school friendships — and left us with just the house and the pines and each other. We talked. We walked sometimes when the snow cleared. She was the one person in Lake Arrowhead I didn't have to explain myself to, the one conversation that didn't require armor. I was counting the months until I could leave. She was the only thing that made the counting bearable.

The geography mirrored the emotional landscape. Houses scattered across mountainsides like isolated thoughts, connected by winding roads that took real effort to travel. Making friends required planning, transportation, and intention. It was easier to just stay home and disappear into books.

I didn't have any goals at all for college. The only goal I had was to get the hell out of the house and get out on my own. I just wanted to leave. I was quietly going insane, almost literally, living with these two loonies who couldn't stop arguing every single day.

The Death of Family

When they moved to the mountain, our family life stopped. Cold. There was no family anymore. There was only the gallery and gift shop. Their entire life centered around that place. Now that I run my own business as a ghostwriter, I understand focusing on the business. When you're self-employed, you don't have much choice.

But when you have a family, that's inexcusable. Before moving, Mom was a member of the PTA, she volunteered at the school, she did activities with us children, and she was actively part of our life. After they started the new business, and especially after we moved, none of that was true anymore.

I'm not sure my parents could even tell you the name of the high school I attended. Dad never looked at another report card. Mom never asked about school. It was always the gallery. Everything was that. What kind of stock would they order. How the season was going. What was the weather going to be like and how would that affect sales.

I became more of an annoyance to him, especially because I wouldn't help, than a child. I never really was his son, as far as I can tell. I was his property. Simple as that.

"You know, a real son would help his father's business," Dad said one morning over coffee.

This was why I avoided eating with my parents, I ate alone, in my room. But I wasn't up to confronting dad, not yet, so I just took it, make the appropriate acknowledgements, and got out of there before it turned into an argument.

"The summer catalog needs to be updated," Mom announced, oblivious to the tension.

And just like that, I was dismissed. Not important enough to fight with when there was business to discuss.

The Escape Hatch

I buried myself in reading. I must have read hundreds of science fiction books, science books, history books, and any other kind of book you can name. I locked myself in my room (figuratively, because my father would never have allowed a lock on the door) and turned pages all day long. I think that's how I kept myself from going insane.

Books became my oxygen. Each page was a step away from the house where parents had forgotten they had children, where business had consumed family, where the only conversations were about inventory and profit margins. In those paperbacks with their cracked spines and yellowed pages, I found worlds where problems had solutions, where heroes faced their demons and won, where the story eventually made sense.

And then it was time for college.

The Reality of Independence

I was shocked, as are most college students, at the price of textbooks. I hear it's gotten far worse, but back then it was pretty bad. College was going to be rough because I still lived at home in Lake Arrowhead. That meant a commute every day going down the mountain in the morning and up the mountain in the evening. Thirty miles each way, mostly along twisty, narrow, crowded highways.

"You could get an apartment near campus," Mom suggested when I complained about the drive.

"With what money?"

"Get a student loan."

"For living expenses? While living at home? That doesn't make sense."

"Then stop complaining about the drive."

Classic parental logic. Offer a solution that wasn't really a solution, then dismiss the problem when the solution didn't work.

The winter was especially bad. Putting on chains, driving through snow, learning the hard way about black ice and how slippery it is, it was a real challenge.

During one of these snowstorms, I thought I could get away without putting on chains. Boy was that a mistake. I was going perhaps twenty miles an hour up the hill, and it was getting dark. I saw a snow plow turn in front of me and slammed on the brakes. What I didn't know, because I was new to this driving thing, was hitting the brakes while on snow and ice is a mistake.

I kept moving forward. The car didn't stop like I expected. It fishtailed, and I slammed right into the snowplow. Or rather, the snow in front of the snowplow. That's probably the only thing that prevented my car from being damaged and me from being hurt. It was embarrassing, though. The snowplow driver was very empathetic and calmed me down.

"You okay, son?" the driver called out as he climbed down from his cab.

"I think so." My hands were shaking on the steering wheel.

"First winter driving?"

"Is it that obvious?"

He laughed. "The panicked look gave it away. Plus the fact that you hit the brakes instead of steering into the slide."

"I didn't know there was a difference."

"Well, now you do. Let me help you get unstuck."

It took twenty minutes to dig my car out of the snowbank. The whole time, the driver (his name was Joe) gave me a crash course in winter driving.

"Ice is like driving on glass," he explained. "You want to think ahead, not react. And always, always carry chains."

"I've got chains in the trunk."

"Then why didn't you use them?"

I shrugged. "Thought I could make it without them."

"Son, that's what everyone thinks right before they slide off the mountain."

The Oil Crisis Comedy

This was also during the oil embargo in the late 1970s. Several Middle Eastern countries decided they were going to mess with oil prices, and there were gas lines going for miles. One day, on the way down from the mountain in the morning, there was a line that stretched along the side of the road. Someone opened his car door, and I took it right off. The door landed a hundred feet away, and I had to stop and face the embarrassment of the situation.

"Oh my God," I said, pulling over and running back to where the man was standing next to his now door-less car. "I am so sorry."

"Well," the man said, looking at his car and then at his door lying in the road, "this is a first."

"I'll pay for it. I'll pay for everything. I have insurance."

"Slow down, son. Let me get a look at you." He was an older man, maybe sixty, with kind eyes and the patient demeanor of someone who'd seen a lot in his life. "You hurt?"

"No, sir. You?"

"I'm fine. Car door's seen better days, though."

Other drivers were getting out of their cars to help move the door out of traffic. One guy shook his head and muttered something about "damn kids," but most people seemed more amused than angry.

"I'm a minister," the man told me as we carried his door to his car. "Pastor Williams from the Baptist church down in San Bernardino."

"I'm really sorry, Pastor Williams. This is my worst nightmare."

"Well, if this is your worst nightmare, you've lived a pretty good life so far." He smiled. "These things happen. What's your name?"

"Richard."

"Well, Richard, I'm not going to call the police, and I'm not going to report this to insurance. Consider it a teaching moment."

"A teaching moment?"

"God has a way of putting people in each other's paths for a reason. Maybe the reason is just to remind an old preacher that grace is something you give, not just something you talk about."

Turns out the man was a preacher. He didn't press any charges and didn't even report it. We talked a bit (I guess he liked me), we put the car door into his car, and I drove away with his blessing. I guess I got lucky. There was no damage to my car other than a few scratches, but he had to replace the door on his car.

The absurdity struck me even then. Here I was, trying to get an education, commuting through gas lines created by international politics I didn't understand, accidentally destroying the property of a man of God who responded with more grace than my own father had ever shown me. The world was clearly insane, but at least some of the insanity was kind.

The Long Descent

Every morning, I drove down that mountain road watching the sun rise over a landscape that should have been beautiful but felt like a cage. Every evening, I drove back up, watching the lights of San Bernardino spread below me like a circuit board, knowing I was heading back to a house where I was invisible except when I was inconvenient.

The routine became meditation. Thirty miles of winding road, steep grades, and hairpin turns that required complete attention. It was the only time during the day when my mind was completely quiet, focused entirely on the immediate task of not driving off a cliff.

College was supposed to be freedom. Instead, it was just a longer leash.

But it was a start. Every day away from the house, every conversation with people who didn't know my parents, every class where I was just another student instead of someone's property, these were small acts of rebellion. I was building an identity separate from the chaos I'd been born into.

I didn't know yet that the skills I was developing (the ability to navigate unpredictable situations, to find refuge in learning, to survive on minimal emotional support) would eventually become my greatest professional assets. I was just trying to get through each day without losing what was left of my sanity.

Every mile down that mountain was a mile away from Crazytown. Every mile back up was a reminder that I wasn't free yet.

But I was learning to count miles. And for the first time, I could see a destination that didn't involve my parents' business or my parents' approval or my parents' money.

I could see a future that was mine.

Chapter 12: College

College was a way out. Not out of education — I'd had plenty of that and wanted no more. Out of the house. Out of my parents' orbit. As long as I was enrolled somewhere, I had a reason to leave every morning and a reason to be somewhere they weren't. Whether I learned anything was secondary. Staying busy and staying out of sight was the plan.

At first, I wanted to be a physics major, until I realized how much math would be involved. I have always hated math and didn't want to choose a career in any of the "hard" sciences like physics or chemistry. After taking a couple of these classes my lack of motivation became obvious, and I switched my major to something more to my liking.

Dr. Young - History Of Western Civilization

Although I took many different courses in college, only a few teachers were outstanding. Outside of the computer courses, Dr. Young was just about the best. He taught History of Western Civilization, and he taught it like no one else.

Most of the class was probably turned off by him because he was controversial. Dr. Young wasn't interested in dates and boring facts. He cared about ideas, motivations, and consequences. He seemed more concerned with whether we understood the subject than whether we'd memorized a bunch of names and dates.

The first day of class, he walked in carrying a thick stack of books and dropped them on his desk with a loud thud.

"How many of you think history is boring?" he asked, looking around the room.

About half the class raised their hands tentatively.

"Good. Honest answer. History is boring when it's taught badly. When it's just a list of dates and dead kings, it's meaningless. But when you understand why people did what they did, when you see the connections between events, when you realize that everything happening today has roots going back centuries..." He paused and grinned. "Well, then it gets interesting."

One student in the back raised her hand. "Are we going to have to memorize dates?"

"Some. But I'm more interested in whether you understand why something happened than when it happened. If you can explain why the Protestant Reformation changed Europe forever, I don't care if you think it started in 1517 or 1520."

This was refreshing. Most of my other professors seemed obsessed with meaningless details.

But Dr. Young's real controversy came when he started talking about the Bible.

"Now, I want to be clear about something," he said during our third week. "We're going to discuss the Bible as a historical document. Not as a religious text, not as a matter of faith, but as a piece of literature that profoundly influenced Western civilization. If that makes you uncomfortable, you should probably drop this class now."

A few students shifted nervously in their seats. I leaned forward, intrigued.

"The Bible as we know it today," Dr. Young continued, "is not the same document that existed two thousand years ago. It's been translated, retranslated, edited, and rewritten multiple times. I can show you evidence that it's been substantially revised at least four times."

A girl named Sarah in the front row raised her hand, her face flushed. "Are you saying the Bible isn't true?"

"I'm saying the Bible is a complex historical document that reflects the political and social concerns of the people who compiled it. The version you read today was shaped by decisions made by church councils, kings, and translators over many centuries."

"That's blasphemy," Sarah said quietly.

"No," Dr. Young replied calmly, "that's scholarship. There's a difference between studying something and attacking it. I'm not telling you what to believe. I'm showing you how a document that shaped Western civilization came to exist in the form we have today."

The class erupted into spirited discussions after that. Sarah and a few other devout students would challenge Dr. Young regularly, but he never got angry or annoyed when students disagreed with him. He seemed to enjoy the debate.

"Richard," he said to me one day after class, "you've been pretty quiet during our Bible discussions. What do you think?"

"I find it interesting," I said. "I'd never thought about the Bible as a historical document before. The idea that it was compiled and edited by people with their own agendas makes sense."

"Exactly. Whether you're religious or not, you can appreciate the historical process. These weren't divine revelations appearing fully formed. These were human beings making conscious decisions about what to include, what to exclude, how to translate difficult passages."

Dr. Young made me think about subjects I'd previously found boring. When he talked about medieval Europe, he didn't just recite facts about kings and battles. He explained how the Black Death changed labor relationships, how the printing press revolutionized information, how trade routes shaped politics.

"Why do you think the Renaissance happened in Italy and not, say, England?" he asked the class one day.

"Because Italy had the money?" someone suggested.

"Partly. But why did Italy have the money?"

"Trade?"

"Right. But what kind of trade, and why Italy?"

He led us through the logic: Italy's geographic position, the Crusades creating demand for Eastern goods, the development of banking, the concentration of wealth in city-states, the patronage system that supported artists and scholars.

"See?" he said. "It's not random. There are reasons why things happen when and where they do. History isn't just one damn thing after another. It's cause and effect, action and reaction."

Dr. Young enjoyed his students and invited comments and criticism. He seemed genuinely interested in what we thought, not just whether we could regurgitate what he'd told us.

"I don't want you to agree with me," he said during one heated discussion about the Crusades. "I want you to think critically about the evidence and reach your own conclusions. If you disagree with me, tell me why. Show me your reasoning."

Dr. Young brought the history of Europe after the dark ages alive for the first time. While I'd always been interested in history, I'd never cared much for that period. Under his teaching, medieval and Renaissance Europe became a story of human ambition, religious conflict, technological innovation, and social change.

"The past isn't dead," he told us during one of his last lectures. "It's not even past. Everything you see around you, every institution, every idea, every conflict, has roots that go back centuries. If you don't understand where we came from, you can't understand where we're going."

Dr. Young was one of the few professors who seemed to remember that education was supposed to be about learning to think, not just memorizing information. He challenged us to question assumptions, to look for underlying causes, to see connections between seemingly unrelated events.

For someone like me, who'd grown up in a house where questioning anything led to trouble, Dr. Young's classroom was a revelation. Here was an adult who not only tolerated questions but encouraged them. He showed me that intellectual curiosity wasn't something to be ashamed of or hide. It was something to be built and celebrated.

Discovering the Computer Lab

During my first semester in college, I signed up for a computer science class on a whim. I'd never seen a computer before and couldn't have cared less about them. The class looked easy, and I figured knowing something about computers might be useful someday.

The class was called BASIC 101. We learned this primitive programming language and had to put in nine hours of lab work on the school's PDP-11/45.

This machine was ancient even then. It had 128 kilobytes of memory, half eaten up by the operating system. Two twenty-megabyte disk drives that looked like washing machines. Twelve hardcopy terminals, two CRT screens, one graphics terminal, and a teletype. Plus one modem for dialing into UC San Bernardino.

I'd never seen anything like it. The thing was huge and beautiful. I fell in love immediately. The first time I typed a program into a terminal, I knew I'd found my calling. Complete accident.

I started spending more time in the computer lab. Soon I was there every free moment. First finishing assignments, then working on extra credit, then writing programs just because I could.

This was the first time in my life I got excited about learning something. The computer lab became my refuge, even more than books had been. Here was a world that made sense. You wrote code, and if it was logical, it worked. If not, it didn't. No mixed messages, no hidden agendas, no emotional warfare disguised as family dinners.

Programming was everything I'd been looking for without knowing it. Creative but logical, complex but precise, infinite possibilities but with absolute rules. The complete opposite of everything I'd grown up with.

The other computer science students were different too. Most were as socially awkward as me, so I finally fit in somewhere. We spoke the same language: logic and problem-solving. We stayed late in the lab not because we had to, but because we wanted to see if we could make our programs do something new, something better.

But computers? Computers were different.

My schedule slowly filled with computer classes and lab work. By the end of my first year, I started building SPRUTL, a utility program designed to replace several standard computer tools.

Second semester, I took MACRO assembly, a complex programming language. My teacher Rick taught the class for extra money while trying to start his own company.

"You're here late again," Mr. James said one evening. He ran the computer department and found me hunched over a terminal at nine o'clock.

"Just trying to get this subroutine to work," I said, not looking up from the screen.

"What's it supposed to do?"

I explained the problem I was solving. He nodded.

"Most students just do the assignment and leave. You're always trying to make it better."

"I like the challenge."

"Good. Real programming isn't about following instructions. It's about solving problems no one has solved before."

He was right.

Trapped in Fire

During college, I commuted every weekday from our house in Lake Arrowhead to college in San Bernardino. The drive down the mountain was scenic and pretty: a long, twisty road through beautiful forests, trees, streams, and wildlife. I loved that drive. It was relaxing.

That summer had been hot and dry for weeks. Fire warnings had been posted, but I wasn't paying attention.

One hot summer day as I was driving down the mountain, I realized the sides of the road were on fire. Trees and shrubs were burning all around me. My stomach dropped. I looked back and saw the fire had jumped the road behind me. I couldn't go that way. I looked ahead. More fire. To my left and right. Fire everywhere.

I was trapped.

At that moment I thought I was going to die. Not someday, not eventually. Right here, right now, burned alive in my car on a mountain road. The terror hit me like a physical blow. My hands started shaking on the steering wheel.

I saw a fireman running toward me through the smoke, radio in hand. Thank God. I stopped and let him into the passenger seat, my heart hammering so hard I could barely think.

"Drive slowly forward," he said.

Forward? Into the fire? But I did what he said while he talked on his radio. A few minutes later, as we were getting close to the wall of flames in front of us, he told me to stop. I had no idea what he was doing. There was fire in all directions. We were going to die here.

Suddenly the car was immersed in water. The world exploded around us. I learned later the fireman had directed me to drive to an open spot on the road, and a helicopter dumped water directly on us. After that, I continued my trip down the mountain, hands still shaking, adrenaline making me feel sick.

The fire turned out to be one of the larger ones in California history. It ruined my scenic drive forever. Instead of beautiful trees, green shrubs, and forest animals, there was blackened earth and burned logs everywhere.

I had been completely unprepared for a disaster of that magnitude. I had no idea what to do or where to go. If I had been paying more attention, I might have avoided being trapped by the fire in the first place.

The lesson I learned was to pay attention to my surroundings. But more than that, I realized I needed to get out of my parents' house and take control of my own life. I couldn't keep depending on other people to save me from situations I should have avoided in the first place.

Bob the Obsessive

Bob was one of the more interesting people I've ever known and became a friend. Not a close one, but as close to a friend as I had in those days. I was so stupidly shy that it's amazing I had any friends at all.

He was shorter than me, heavier (though not obese), with brown hair, perpetual acne, and a nose that never stopped running. Despite all this, Bob had infectious enthusiasm that could make the most mundane technical details sound like the secrets of the universe.

I met Bob in the computer lab where he worked as a student aide. The first time I saw him, he was hunched over a terminal, completely absorbed in whatever he was coding. When he finally looked up, his eyes lit up like he'd found a fellow traveler.

"You're the guy who's been living in here, right?" he said, pushing his glasses up his nose. "I've seen your programs. That sorting algorithm you wrote is pretty elegant."

That's how conversations with Bob started. No small talk, no weather commentary. Just immediate deep dives into whatever technical obsession was consuming him that day. For someone as painfully shy as me, this was perfect. We could talk for hours about computers and games without navigating the terrifying waters of normal social interaction.

Bob was obsessed with two things: Dungeons & Dragons and AlphaMicro computers. He was willing to share these obsessions with someone who listened.

"Have you ever heard of AlphaMicro?" he asked me one day, his voice filled with reverence most people reserved for religious experiences.

"No, what's that?"

"Only the most elegant computer architecture ever designed," he said, pulling out a thick manual.

I was probably the only person in the computer lab who would sit still while Bob explained the technical specifications of machines that looked like beige refrigerators. But I found his enthusiasm interesting, and he seemed grateful to have someone who didn't walk away when he started talking about multi-user operating systems.

Bob's real obsession was D&D, and this became the foundation of our friendship.

"Okay, forget computers for a minute," he said one afternoon, spreading a hand-drawn map across the lab table. "Look at this."

The map was incredibly detailed. Not just continents and cities, but trade routes, political boundaries, climate zones, even migration patterns of fantasy creatures.

"This is Valdris," he said, pointing to a kingdom in the center. "Constitutional monarchy, population about 2.3 million, primary exports are textiles and enchanted weapons."

I stared at the map, fascinated not just by the detail but by the fact that Bob trusted me enough to share something he'd clearly spent enormous amounts of time creating.

"You made this up?"

"Made it up?" Bob looked genuinely offended. "I've been developing this world for three years."

For someone as socially awkward as me, having Bob explain his fantasy worlds was like finding a safe space. We were both geeks. We both understood obsessive attention to detail. Neither of us had to pretend to be normal.

"Do you want to play?" he asked, eyes bright with hope.

The honest answer was no. The idea of sitting around a table with other people, even other geeks, pretending to be a fantasy character, terrified me. But I didn't want to hurt Bob's feelings.

"Could I just read your materials? All of them?"

Bob practically glowed. "You want to read my world-building notes?"

"All of them."

He showed up the next day with a stack of notebooks six inches thick. Maps, character descriptions, political treatises, religious doctrines, historical timelines. But the real treasure was when he handed me a typed document titled "D&D Dirty Tricks."

"I wrote this for other Dungeon Masters," he said proudly. "It's 1800 traps and situations designed to target characters with maximum statistics."

Bob had weaponized game mechanics. He'd turned players' strengths into weaknesses through pure systematic thinking. It was brilliant and completely obsessive in the way only true geeks could appreciate.

Reading Bob's materials triggered something in me I didn't expect. I became obsessed with collecting every D&D book, every module, every variant, every other role-playing game I could find. I had to own them all. The irony? I never played the games. Not once.

"There's this new supplement coming out," Bob would tell me excitedly. "Oriental Adventures."

"I need it," I'd say immediately.

"But we're not even using Oriental rules in my campaign."

"Doesn't matter. I need it anyway."

Bob understood because he was the same way. We were both collectors, systematizers, people who needed to understand how things worked and fit together. We were both social misfits who'd found something we could talk about without the usual awkwardness.

Our friendship was built around shared obsessions instead of normal social bonding. We never hung out outside the computer lab. We never talked about personal stuff. But for a few hours each day, we had someone who understood our particular brand of geekiness.

"You know what I love about these games?" Bob said one day, surrounded by our respective piles of manuals. "They're like programming, but for entire worlds."

He was right. We weren't interested in playing games or making friends the normal way. We were interested in understanding systems, in having comprehensive knowledge of things other people thought were weird, and in finding someone else who got it.

I only knew Bob during my college years. After I dropped out, I lost contact with him, though I did spot him a couple of times at Renaissance Faires. He was usually dressed as some elaborate fantasy character, probably still explaining game mechanics to anyone who'd listen.

For someone as shy as I was, Bob represented something rare: friendship based on shared interests instead of social skills. He introduced me to systematic collecting that would consume years of my life, but he showed me it was possible to connect with another person without having to be someone I wasn't.

Thanks to Bob, I spent the next several years accumulating an embarrassingly complete collection of role-playing materials I never used. But I learned that friendship could exist in the spaces between normal social interaction, built on mutual obsession and the relief of finding someone equally weird.

Daniel - Computer Genius

One day I was sitting in the computer lab, staring at my screen in frustration. I'd been wrestling with this programming assignment for hours, and nothing was working. The code looked right to me, but the compiler kept spitting out error messages I couldn't understand.

A somewhat portly young man wandered over and peered at my screen.

"Having trouble?" he asked.

"This stupid program won't compile," I said. "I've checked the syntax a dozen times, and I can't figure out what's wrong."

He leaned closer and studied my code for maybe thirty seconds. "There," he said, pointing to a line. "You've got a semicolon where you need a comma. And down here, you're missing a closing brace."

I looked where he was pointing. He was right. Two tiny errors that had been driving me crazy for hours, and he spotted them in half a minute.

"Thanks," I said. "I'm Richard."

"Daniel. But everyone calls me Dan."

During the next few months, I got to know Dan well. He was a lab assistant whose job was to keep the computer operating, make sure the printers had paper, and help students with their projects. But Dan was way overqualified for that kind of work.

I learned to admire and respect him. Dan was one of the most intelligent people I'd ever met, and he was brilliant at programming. More than that, he had something most programmers lacked: style.

"Look at this," he said one day, showing me some code a student had written. "Technically, it works. But it's a mess. Variable names like 'X1' and 'TEMP2' that tell you nothing. No comments explaining what anything does. Indentation all over the place."

"But it works, right?"

"Sure, it works. But what happens six months from now when you need to modify it? Or when someone else has to maintain it? Good programming isn't just about making the computer understand your code. It's about making humans understand it too."

Dan taught me about elegant programming. He showed me how to choose meaningful variable names, how to structure code so it was readable, how to write comments that explained not just what the code did, but why it did it.

"Programming is communication," he told me. "You're not just talking to the computer. You're talking to the next programmer who has to work with your code. Maybe that programmer is you, three years from now, trying to remember what the hell you were thinking."

Dan's masterpiece was a program called DKCLN that he wrote for the computer lab. The PDP-11's disk drives were constantly running out of space, and the lab assistants spent hours manually hunting down files to delete.

"Watch this," Dan said, running his program. DKCLN scanned the entire disk system, identified old temporary files, duplicate files, and abandoned student projects, then presented everything in a neat report.

"It finds all the junk automatically?" I asked.

"More than that. It categorizes everything by age, size, and usage patterns. See these files here? They haven't been accessed in six months and they're taking up huge amounts of space. These over here are temporary files that students forgot to clean up. And this whole directory belongs to a guy who graduated two years ago."

I studied the program's output, then looked at the source code. It was beautiful. Every function had a clear purpose, every variable had a descriptive name, every section was documented.

"This is incredible," I said. "You've automated the whole cleanup process."

"That's what computers are for," Dan replied. "Why should humans spend time doing tedious work that machines can do better?"

That was my introduction to systems programming. After examining DKCLN, I became convinced that the future lay in writing utilities to help people operate computer systems more efficiently.

Dan and I started spending countless hours together, working day and night to solve obscure programming problems. He had this way of breaking down complex issues into manageable pieces.

"Okay," he'd say when I brought him a nasty bug, "let's think about this systematically. What's the program supposed to do? What's it doing? Where's the disconnect?"

He'd walk me through debugging techniques, show me how to trace through code execution, teach me to think like the computer.

"The machine is never wrong," he'd remind me. "If your program isn't working, it's because you told it to do something other than what you think you told it to do."

Taking Dan's cue, I became a lab assistant myself, earning $3.25 an hour. I started helping students during evening hours, and it boosted my self-image. For the first time in my life, people were coming to me for help with technical problems.

"Richard," Dan said one evening as we were closing up the lab, "you've gotten good at this. You're explaining things better than some of the professors."

"I learned from the best," I said.

"You've got a knack for breaking complex ideas down into simple pieces. That's a rare skill."

Dan had this gift for making me feel competent. In a world where I usually felt awkward and out of place, the computer lab became a sanctuary where I could help people solve problems.

"You know what I like about programming?" Dan said during one of our late-night sessions. "It's one of the few places where being a perfectionist is useful. The computer doesn't care if you're socially awkward or if you don't fit in. It only cares if your logic is correct."

After Dan graduated, he moved to San Jose, about 450 miles away. We lost contact except for occasional phone calls where he'd tell me about his new job and ask how things were going at school.

"I'm working for this company that makes database software," he told me during one call. "We're building systems that can handle thousands of users simultaneously."

"That sounds amazing. Are you using the same principles you taught me?"

"Absolutely. Clean code, clear documentation, elegant solutions. Turns out the real world needs that stuff even more than the computer lab did."

We managed to get together once when I visited San Francisco for a seminar. Dan looked the same, but he was wearing a suit and talking about corporate strategy and market positioning.

"You've changed," I told him over lunch.

"The work is different," he admitted. "More management, less hands-on programming. But the fundamentals are the same. You still have to solve problems systematically, you still have to communicate clearly, you still have to think about the human beings who will use what you build."

That was the last time I saw him. We lost contact completely after that. Last I heard, he was working his way up the corporate ladder at some large tech company.

But Dan's influence on my thinking lasted long after he disappeared from my life. He taught me that technical skill without communication ability was useless. He showed me that programming was as much about human psychology as computer science. He demonstrated that being smart and capable could earn you respect, even if you didn't fit the typical social mold.

Dan was proof that geeks could succeed in the real world, not by changing who they were, but by getting good at what they did.

Rick - MACRO Class

The MACRO class was much more interesting than anything I'd taken before. MACRO is a computer language of sorts, but unlike FORTRAN and BASIC where you have simple commands like PRINT or LET, MACRO makes you code each machine instruction individually.

"Think of it this way," Rick explained on the first day of class. "When you type PRINT in BASIC, you're like a general giving orders to his army. You say 'take that hill' and hundreds of soldiers execute the order. In MACRO, you're commanding each individual soldier. You have to tell each one exactly where to step, when to fire, how to reload."

Rick was my MACRO teacher, and he was impossible to miss. In stocking feet, Rick stood six feet, eleven inches tall. He towered over everyone, and his booming, cheerful voice could be heard throughout the entire computer science building.

"Now, some of you are probably thinking, 'Why would I want to do all that extra work?'" Rick continued, grinning at the class. "That's like asking why a race car driver would want to know how an engine works instead of just turning the key. When you program in MACRO, you understand what's really happening inside the machine."

Rick was a teacher who taught one class a week to make extra money while starting his new company. At the time, he called it Systems Associates, though he later renamed it Software Techniques.

"I'm not here because I need the money," he told us during his introduction. "Well, okay, I do need the money. But I'm really here because I love this stuff. I love programming, I love computers, and I love talking about both."

That was an understatement. Rick loved to talk, and he could talk for hours about practically anything, especially himself.

Before becoming a teacher, Rick had worked for Digital Equipment Corporation as a service representative. When customers had problems with DEC machines, Rick was the guy they called.

"I was the best service rep DEC had," Rick told us matter-of-factly. "Not to brag, but my supervisor Mike used to say I could fix machines that other guys couldn't even diagnose. I had customers who would refuse to work with anyone else."

"How did you get so good?" one student asked.

"I didn't just learn the manuals," Rick said, his eyes lighting up. "I lived and breathed those machines. I'd take them apart in my garage, rebuild them, modify them. Other guys would follow the troubleshooting flowcharts. I'd listen to the sounds the drives made, feel the vibrations in the chassis, watch the patterns on the oscilloscope. These machines have personalities, and once you understand their personalities, you can make them sing."

Rick had a tendency to exaggerate, but his enthusiasm was infectious. He'd describe debugging a complex system failure like he was narrating an epic battle.

"So there I was at this customer site," he said during one lecture, "three in the morning, and their entire payroll system was down. The computer was making this grinding noise that sounded like a dying elephant. Every other tech had given up, said the machine was toast. But I knew that sound. I'd heard it before."

He paused dramatically, looking around the classroom.

"What was it?" someone asked.

"Bad bearing in the disk drive motor. Took me four hours to replace it, but I saved their entire payroll database. The customer was so grateful, they sent a case of champagne to my office."

Rick felt stifled at DEC and decided to leave the company. He was well prepared for the transition.

"I didn't just quit," he told us. "I walked out with a dozen customers who followed me to my new company. These weren't just accounts, they were relationships. They trusted me, not DEC. And you know why? Because I could solve their problems, and I could explain things in ways they could understand."

"How did you convince them to switch?" I asked.

"I didn't have to convince them," Rick replied with a grin. "They convinced themselves. When you consistently solve people's problems and make their lives easier, they want to work with you. It's not about selling them something. It's about being useful."

Rick's lectures were great because he could spice up even the driest technical material with personal anecdotes and war stories from his DEC days.

"Now, when you're writing MACRO code," he'd say, "you have to think like the processor. The processor is like a very literal-minded employee. It will do exactly what you tell it to do, nothing more, nothing less. I once had a customer whose program was running perfectly except it kept printing paychecks for negative amounts. Turns out the programmer had made one tiny error in how he handled signed numbers. The computer was doing exactly what it was told, but what it was told was wrong."

He'd demonstrate concepts using elaborate analogies that somehow made complex assembly language operations seem logical and even elegant.

"Memory allocation is like organizing a warehouse," he explained. "You need to know where everything is stored, how much space each item takes up, and how to find things quickly when you need them. MACRO lets you be the warehouse manager instead of just a customer placing orders."

The small program Rick had us write first was deceptively simple. All it did was load some numbers into memory and then die with an error. But the error message would print out the values we'd stored in those memory locations.

"It's not much to look at," Rick admitted, "but you've just written your first program that talks directly to the hardware. You've told the processor exactly what to do, step by step. That makes you more than a programmer. That makes you a systems architect."

Rick had this gift for making every small accomplishment feel significant. He understood that learning MACRO was intimidating, and he made sure we felt proud of even the tiniest victories.

"Programming in MACRO is like learning to speak directly to the machine," he told us. "Most programmers never get this close to the hardware. You're joining an elite group of people who understand what's really happening inside these boxes."

Whether or not that was true, Rick made us believe it. And that belief made all the difference in how we approached the challenges ahead.

DECUS

Don was one of my best friends in college. We both majored in computer science, talked constantly, and spent hours on programming projects. Don could make the most complex algorithms sound like casual conversation.

One day Don came up to me grinning. "You're not going to believe this. Rick's sending me to DECUS."

"What the hell is DECUS?"

"Digital Equipment Corporation User's Society. Imagine all the gods of programming coming down from Mount Olympus to teach mortals their secrets."

I stared at him. "You mean the people who built these machines?"

"The very ones. Four days in San Diego. Seminars run by the creators of the computers we live on."

I felt that familiar stab of jealousy mixed with desperate want. "How much does something like that cost?"

Don rattled off numbers that might as well have been the national debt. I was completely broke, living on ramen and hope.

An idea hit me. "You know, expenses wouldn't be much higher for two people than one. We could share a room, eat cheap..."

Don looked at me sideways. "You want to come?"

"Are you kidding? I'd kill to meet these people."

He pulled out a crumpled piece of paper and started doing math. Scribbling numbers, crossing things out, adding it up again. Finally he looked up. "If you drive and we split gas, Rick's money should cover both of us. Barely."

"Deal."

The four-day symposium was in San Diego. I packed my only suit (a threadbare thing I'd inherited from someone) planning to wear it all four days. Along with dress shoes that pinched and the usual necessities.

The morning we left, I was so excited I could barely sleep. We hit the road at 4 a.m., driving through the darkness while Don dozed in the passenger seat. By the time we reached our hotel at 7 a.m., I was running on pure adrenaline.

"God, we look like refugees," Don said, checking us both in the lobby mirror.

"Speak for yourself. I look distinguished."

"You look like you slept in a car."

"Because I did sleep in a car."

We registered, threw our stuff in the room, and headed straight to the convention center. The moment I walked in, I knew I was home. Everywhere I looked, people were talking about code, algorithms, system architecture. These weren't just programmers. These were the architects of the digital world I'd fallen in love with.

For four straight days, I haunted every seminar I could find. I sat in the front row, took notes like my life depended on it, and asked probably way too many questions. Don would find me at lunch hunched over my notebook, scribbling down everything I could remember.

"You realize you're allowed to eat, right?" he'd say.

"Food is temporary. This knowledge is forever."

The peak moment came on day three when I spotted Rick across the room. He was hobbling around on a cast, and when he saw us, he limped over with a big grin.

"Don! How are you enjoying your first DECUS?"

"It's incredible," Don said. "This is my friend Richard, the one I told you about."

Rick looked me up and down. "Ah, the one who's been living in the computer lab."

"Guilty as charged."

"What happened to your leg?" Don asked.

Rick laughed. "Pure stupidity. I was chasing Kirby Altman down some stairs at the hotel yesterday and took a tumble. Broke my damn leg." He shifted his weight on the cast. "Speaking of Kirby, you guys want to come up to my room? He's there now, and I think you'd enjoy meeting him."

Did I want to meet Kirby Altman? The Kirby Altman? I tried to play it cool. "Sure, that sounds interesting."

Rick's hotel room was chaos. Papers everywhere, code printouts scattered across the bed, empty coffee cups on every surface. And there, sitting cross-legged on the floor with a stack of computer printouts, was Kirby Altman.

"Kirby, meet Don and Richard. These are the college kids I was telling you about."

Kirby looked up and grinned. "The ones living on ramen and dedication?"

"That's us," I said.

For the next two hours, we talked code. Kirby showed us some of his latest work: elegant, beautiful programs that made my efforts look like finger painting. But instead of making me feel inadequate, it inspired me. This was what was possible. This was the level I wanted to reach.

"The thing about programming," Kirby said at one point, "is that anyone can write code that works. The art is writing code that sings."

I knew exactly what he meant.

When it was time to leave San Diego, Don and I loaded up the car with notes, brochures, promotional buttons, stickers, and enough technical documentation to start our own library. The drive home felt different. Longer, somehow. Like we were traveling back from a different world.

"That was unreal," Don said somewhere around Oceanside.

"I know exactly what I want to do with my life now," I said.

"What's that?"

"I want to write code that sings."

Of all the computer conventions I've attended since (and there have been many), that first DECUS remains my favorite. It wasn't just about the technical knowledge, though that was incredible. It was about finding my people, my tribe, my future. I'd spent my whole life feeling like I didn't fit anywhere. But in those hotel conference rooms full of programmers and system architects, I finally found home.

The Breaking Point

Two incidents that summer changed everything between my father and me forever. The first one happened on a Tuesday afternoon in the kitchen.

I was standing at the counter, making a sandwich or getting something to drink, when my father snuck up behind me and grabbed me in a bear hug. He was probably just kidding around, trying to be playful in his awkward way.

I spun around, anger exploding through me like a lightning bolt. For a split second, I saw myself at six years old, looking in the bathroom mirror with that same rage burning in my eyes. The same helpless fury I'd felt as a little kid, except now I wasn't helpless anymore.

I dropped into a fighting stance, fists up, ready to swing.

My father saw my face and started to laugh. "Jesus, Richard, I was just..."

Then he realized I wasn't kidding. I was dead serious. Ready to kill him or be killed trying. The laughter died in his throat.

"Never touch me again," I said, my voice shaking with rage. "Ever."

He stepped back, hands raised. "Okay, okay. Christ, what's wrong with you?"

I didn't answer. I just stood there, fists still clenched, staring at him until he left the kitchen. Something fundamental had shifted. I wasn't his little boy anymore. I wasn't anyone's victim.

The second incident happened about a month later. I was in my room with the door shut, reading Heinlein's "The Moon Is a Harsh Mistress." I loved that book: the story of a lunar colony's revolution against Earth's oppressive rule. Freedom through rebellion. The theme felt relevant to my life.

I heard my father's voice from the family room: "Richard, go upstairs and get me a glass of wine."

That was it. I'd had enough of being a slave in my own house. Without thinking, I yelled back: "Why don't you get off your ass, you fat fuck, and get your own fucking wine?"

The silence that followed was deafening.

Then all hell broke loose.

"WHAT DID YOU SAY TO ME?" he roared, his footsteps thundering down the hallway toward my room.

I threw my book aside and stood up, adrenaline flooding my system. "You heard me."

He burst through my door, his face purple with rage. "You little shit! How dare you talk to me like that!"

"How dare I? How about how dare you treat me like your personal servant!"

"I'm your father! You live in my house!"

"Your house? You mean the house where I get ordered around like a slave? Where nobody talks to me unless they need something done?"

We stood there screaming at each other, faces inches apart. For a moment, I thought we were going to throw punches.

Part of me wanted to. Part of me was ready to finish what we'd started in the kitchen.

The shouting match went on for what felt like hours. My mother appeared in the doorway at some point, looking terrified, but neither of us paid any attention to her. This was between him and me, and it had been building for years.

Finally, breathing hard, my father stepped back and delivered his ultimatum: "If you don't like the rules, you can leave."

"Fine," I shot back. "Maybe I will."

"Good. I'll help you pack."

"Good."

We glared at each other for another few seconds, then he turned and walked away.

I sat back down on my bed, my hands still shaking. That fit into my plans perfectly. It was time to go, by whatever means necessary. I even considered finding a friend and sleeping on their couch. I probably could have stayed at Dan's place, but I never put that into action.

From that moment on, in my father's eyes, I was a mortal enemy. He wanted one thing: for me to move out. I wanted one thing: to get the hell out.

The cold war had begun. We barely spoke after that, and when we did, it was purely functional. "Dinner's ready." "I'm going out." "Close the door." The house felt like a demilitarized zone with two hostile armies occupying the same territory.

My mother tried to pretend nothing had happened, but the tension was impossible to ignore. She'd look from him to me during the few meals we shared, her face anxious, as if she expected us to start throwing punches over the mashed potatoes.

I'd crossed a line I could never uncross. I'd stood up to him, called him out, refused to back down. There was no going back to the way things were, and I didn't want to go back. I was done being afraid of him. Done being that same helpless child he'd molested when I was six years old.

I realized this was a life or death situation. Either he was going to kill me, or I was going to kill him. It got that bad. We couldn't be in the same house anymore without the risk of real violence. I knew that one more confrontation, one more moment of him trying to assert his dominance or me refusing to back down, could push us both over the edge. Something had to give, and soon, or one of us wasn't going to walk away from the next fight.

Now I just needed to figure out how to escape before one of us did something we'd both regret.

The countdown to my independence or extreme violence had begun.

Desperate to Escape

Earning a living and getting an education took on new urgency as the situation at home grew unbearable. My parents and I barely spoke anymore. When my father did address me, it was just commands: "Take out the trash." "Mow the lawn." "Clean up this mess." No conversations, no questions about school, no interest in what I was doing with my life.

The house had become frostily cold. My mother would nod when I walked into a room, maybe mumble "dinner's ready" if I was lucky. Most of the time, we moved around each other like strangers sharing space in a boarding house. The silence was worse than fighting.

I'd sit at the dinner table, pushing food around my plate while they ate in complete silence. The only sounds were forks scraping against plates and the occasional "pass the salt." I felt invisible.

The forest fire that had nearly killed me made everything worse. I didn't want to be doing this anymore. Living at home, depending on people who treated me like a burden, driving down a mountain every day where fires could trap me again. I needed out fast.

I saved every penny from my lab assistant job, calculating and recalculating how much I'd need for moving expenses, deposits, and the first few months of rent. I started going out on interviews with anyone who would see me.

At first my sights were set pathetically low. I interviewed at Castle Park, a video game arcade down in Riverside.

"So you want to work at an arcade," the manager said, looking skeptical. "Most college kids think this is just playing games all day."

"I understand it's a business," I replied. "I know about computers and electronics. I could help maintain the machines."

"The pay is minimum wage. You sure you want to work here instead of focusing on school?"

I wanted to tell him that anything was better than the silent treatment at home, but instead I just nodded. "I need the job."

I interviewed with department stores, shopping centers, insurance companies. Anywhere that might pay enough to support basic survival. My plan was simple: get any job, move out, finish my education, then get a real job with a computer company. The first priority was escaping that cold, silent house where I felt like a ghost.

But none of these jobs paid enough. Even working full-time at minimum wage, I couldn't afford rent, food, and tuition. The math just didn't work.

My friend Don made everything worse.

"Guess what?" Don said one afternoon, grinning like he'd won the lottery. "I got a job."

"Where?"

"CMC Water District. Rick got it for me. I'm going to be a computer operator."

I felt like someone had punched me in the stomach. "Rick? Our MACRO teacher Rick?"

"Yeah, he knows some guy who works there. They need someone who understands computers. The pay is incredible."

Don told me the salary. It was more than twice what any of my interviews had offered. More than enough to live independently and still go to school.

"That's amazing," I managed to say, but inside I was dying. Don always seemed to be one step ahead of me. While I was begging for minimum wage jobs, he'd landed exactly the kind of position I was dreaming about.

After a few months of fruitless searching, I realized this might be harder than I thought. I had plenty of job offers, but none of them even approached the amount of money I needed to escape. I got frustrated and even considered abandoning my search entirely.

The atmosphere at home wasn't helping. The three of us would sit in the living room watching television, not speaking, not acknowledging each other's existence. I felt like I was slowly disappearing.

I kept looking and searching. It was a rough time and my temper was getting shorter. I had things to accomplish, goals to reach, and nothing seemed to be turning out the way I wanted it.

"You seem angry all the time," Don observed one day in the computer lab.

"I'm frustrated," I said. "You got your break. Where's mine?"

"It'll happen. You just have to be patient."

"Patient?" I snapped. "I've been patient. I've been applying everywhere, interviewing with everyone, and I'm still stuck living in a house where nobody talks to me."

Don looked uncomfortable. "That bad?"

"We don't have conversations. We have nothing. I come home from school, eat dinner in silence, and go to my room. It's like living with robots."

The truth was, I was desperate. Not just for a job, but for proof that I had a future beyond that silent, cold house. The fire had shown me how quickly everything could end. I needed to start living my life before something else happened to stop me.

Then one day, out of the blue, came the call I was hoping for.

I was sitting in the computer lab, working on an assignment, when someone tapped me on the shoulder.

"Richard? There's a phone call for you at the front desk."

I walked to the front desk, wondering who could be calling me at school. My parents never called. They barely spoke to me when I was standing right next to them.

"This is Richard."

"Richard, this is Rick. Rick from your MACRO class. Do you have a minute to talk?"

My heart started pounding. "Sure. What's up?"

"I might have a job opportunity for you. Are you still looking for work?"

"Absolutely."

"Good. Can you come to my office tomorrow afternoon? I'd like you to meet some people."

"What kind of job?" I asked, trying to keep my voice steady.

"Computer programming. Real programming, not data entry or computer operator stuff. Are you interested?"

I nearly dropped the phone. "Yes. Definitely yes."

"Great. I'll see you tomorrow at two o'clock."

I hung up the phone and just stood there for a moment, afraid to believe it was real. After months of rejection and disappointment, after watching Don get everything I wanted, after living in that frozen house where I felt like I didn't exist, maybe it was finally my turn.

My life was about to change completely.

The Call That Changed Everything

Rick was the same person who had taught the assembly language class the previous semester. By now, he had started a small consulting company with two partners, Steve Davis and Steve Edwards. They provided custom programming and support to about a dozen clients, including CMC Water District.

The workload was becoming too much for just the three of them, so they decided to hire their first employee. This was a huge step since up to that time they were only responsible for themselves.

They had two other pressing reasons to hire someone: they wanted health insurance (most group plans required a minimum of four people) and they needed the tax write-offs. Having an employee would also lend an air of respectability to their young, struggling company.

They would have hired Don, but they'd just placed him at CMC Water District. It would have looked terrible if they turned around and hired him themselves. Instead, they asked Don if he knew anyone else who might be interested. Don recommended me, and Rick asked him to give me a call.

That phone call from Don changed the course of my life. I still remember that conversation like it was yesterday.

The phone rang while I was sitting in my room, trying to focus on homework while the tension in the house pressed down on me like a weight.

"Hi," Don said when I picked up. "Remember me?"

"Of course, stupid," I replied. "We were just together last week."

"Yeah, yeah. Boy, have I got news for you. You're going to love me. You're going to die."

My heart started beating faster. "Well, why don't you spit it out?"

"Rick, you remember Rick? He started his own company called Software Techniques. Well, they need to hire someone quickly, someone willing to work for peanuts. When Rick mentioned this to me, I told him all about you."

I was stunned. Speechless. For several moments I couldn't even breathe. This was it. This was my escape route.

"Tell Rick I'd like to talk with him," I finally managed to say, my voice quivering.

"Better yet," Don said, "why don't you call him yourself? Here's his phone number."

I called Rick immediately, and we set up an interview for the next day at his apartment in Orange County.

Rick's place was huge, a sprawling apartment that felt more like a house. When Dorothy, his girlfriend, answered the door, I could see the living room stretched out behind her with comfortable couches arranged around a coffee table. Computer manuals and printouts were scattered everywhere.

"You must be Richard," Dorothy said with a warm smile. "Come on in. Rick's expecting you, and Steve and Steve should be here any minute."

"Thanks," I said, trying not to seem too nervous.

Rick appeared from what looked like a home office. "Richard! Great to see you again. How was the drive?"

"Not too bad, once I figured out the freeway system," I said.

"Good, good. Have a seat. Dorothy, could you get Richard something to drink?"

"What would you like?" Dorothy asked. "We have Coke, 7-Up, coffee..."

"Coke would be great," I said, settling into one of the couches.

The apartment was impressive. Floor-to-ceiling windows, expensive-looking furniture, and what seemed like every computer manual ever published. This was where serious money was being made.

Steve Davis and Steve Edwards arrived exactly on time. Steve Davis was tall and thin with wire-rimmed glasses, very serious and methodical. Steve Edwards was shorter and stockier, with a more relaxed demeanor but sharp eyes that seemed to take in everything.

"So, you're the programmer Don's been telling us about," Steve Davis said, shaking my hand.

"That's me," I replied. "I brought some of my code to show you."

"Excellent," Steve Edwards said. "We'd love to see what you've been working on."

Dorothy appeared with a tray of sodas and some crackers and cheese. "I thought you might want some snacks while you talk," she said.

I pulled out my SPRUTL program listings: carefully organized pages of assembly code that I'd spent months perfecting.

"This is my main project from last semester," I said, spreading the printouts on the coffee table. "It's a utility program that replaces several standard system tools."

Steve Davis picked up the first few pages and started scanning through them. His eyebrows went up.

"This is very clean code," he said to his partners. "Look at this commenting structure."

Steve Edwards leaned over to look. "And the variable naming is excellent. You can understand what the program does just by reading it."

Rick was grinning. "I told you guys he was good."

"Where did you learn to document code like this?" Steve Davis asked me.

"I had a friend named Dan who taught me that programming is communication," I said. "You're not just talking to the computer, you're talking to the next programmer who has to maintain your code."

"Exactly right," Steve Edwards said, nodding approvingly. "Most programmers never figure that out."

They spent the next twenty minutes going through my code, asking questions about specific functions and design decisions. I could tell they were impressed. They kept exchanging meaningful looks and nodding.

"This is exactly the kind of programming we need," Steve Davis said. "Systematic, well-documented, maintainable code."

"The question is," Steve Edwards said, "are you ready to work in a real business environment? This isn't just writing programs for class anymore."

"I'm ready," I said. "I want to learn how to build systems that people use."

Rick was bouncing in his chair. "See? I told you he had the right attitude."

The three partners stepped into the kitchen for a few minutes to discuss my candidacy. I sat there trying not to fidget, sipping my Coke and pretending to study the computer manuals on the coffee table.

Dorothy sat down across from me. "Don't worry," she said quietly. "Rick wants to hire you. He's been talking about it since you called."

When they came back, all three were smiling.

"We'd like to offer you a position," Rick said. "Can you start soon?"

"How soon?" I asked.

"How about next week?"

I tried not to seem too eager. "That sounds perfect."

They told me they'd call me the next day with the details, and I left feeling like I was floating on air. I'd done it. I'd impressed them. I was going to be a professional programmer.

The Offer and the Great Escape

The next morning, at 8:00 AM, I called Rick. I couldn't wait any longer. I had to know if I had a job. He was already awake, working on a terminal in his apartment.

"Well Rick," I asked, somewhat boldly, "did you like me? Did I get the job?"

"Sure," he said. "We're offering $12,000 a year."

My heart nearly stopped. This was much more than I would have settled for. I was only making $5,000 a year at Jensen's Market. I estimated that, with a roommate, I could easily survive on that amount.

"Sounds great," I said, trying to keep my voice steady. "When can I start?"

"How about tomorrow?" Rick replied.

"Oh, that's a bit close. I need to quit my current job and find an apartment down in your area. Why don't I start on Monday." Monday was five days away. I figured that would be plenty of time.

"Fine. Show up at my apartment on Monday at 8:00."

I felt on top of the world. I was happy! Finally, I could leave home. The world would be mine to conquer.

Of course, there were a few details to work out first. I had to find a roommate, rent an apartment, move, drop out of college, and quit my job at Jensen's Market.

Finding a roommate turned out to be easy. I called Don to tell him the news, which he already knew.

"Yeah, Rick called me and told me last night," he said. "He thought you were great."

"Oh. Now I've got to find a place in Orange County," I said.

"Well," Don began, "are you looking for a roommate?"

"As a matter of fact..." I began.

"I thought so. Just so happens that I want to move a bit closer to work myself. This one-hour commute is killing me."

"Great, let's look for apartments this weekend," I said, very happy with the way things were turning out.

Next on the agenda was quitting my job. My boss Mike was a nice guy, but he had a habit that I hated. Whenever he fired someone, he didn't give them any notice or severance pay. He was perfectly consistent about it - he never gave anyone this benefit.

Because of this, I didn't see any reason not to return the favor. I had no plans to return to that job, so I didn't see any need to keep that bridge intact.

I decided to quit that morning.

As soon as Mike saw me, he knew something was wrong. I was grinning broadly from ear to ear.

"You look like the cat who just ate the canary," he said.

"I'm on top of the world," I said.

"Why?"

"Well, I just got an offer for another job, a very good job, and I've decided to accept."

"Oh," Mike said, "when do you start?"

"Monday," I said. "Next Monday, in fact."

Mike's face turned red as a beet. He said, coldly, "You're leaving without giving me any notice?"

"Well," I said to him, "I noticed that when you fired Kim, you didn't give her severance. In fact, you've never given anyone even a day's severance. I figured it was time to show you how it felt."

Mike turned away. I could see the muscles in his arms tensing up. The veins on his neck were popping out and throbbing. This man was angry!

"You owe me two weeks notice," he said.

"You goddamn son-of-a-bitch. You expect two weeks notice from me? After never giving notice to anyone? How does it feel, asshole?" I said, matter-of-factly.

He didn't say anything for a minute. He looked like he was attempting to get his anger under control.

"Fine. Your final paycheck will be in the office in ten minutes," he said, anger seething from his voice.

"Thanks," I said.

He didn't say anything, and I left. I walked upstairs to the office to pick up my final check. The office girl was busy typing it up for me.

"What did you say to Mike?" she asked. "He was so angry I thought he was going to attack me through the phone."

I explained what happened, and she laughed. She loved it! Finally, someone got back at Mike.

The most painful task left was dropping out of college. I didn't feel too badly about it, since I'd decided college was pretty worthless to me. I was just continuing because there didn't seem to be anything better to do.

Mr. James, the head of the computer science department, was flabbergasted. I think he saw me as his star pupil. The thought of my dropping out came as a bitter blow to him.

"Why don't you continue your education at night?" he asked.

"No way. I've achieved my goal. I've gotten a job in a good, solid field. I may come back to college in a couple of years, after I've gotten some experience."

I think both of us knew that was a lie the moment I said it. There was no way I'd ever come back to school, and Mr. James knew it.

But I didn't care. I was free. Free from my parents' house, free from the cold war with my father, free to start my real life. In five days, I'd be a professional programmer living on my own.

The countdown to independence was over. My new life was about to begin.

Moving Day

Finding an apartment turned out to be surprisingly easy. Don and I sat at his kitchen table one Saturday morning, circling ads in the Orange County Register classified section.

"Here's one," Don said, pointing to a small ad. "Garden Grove, two bedroom, $325 a month."

"That's not bad," I said, doing quick math in my head. "Split two ways, that's only $162.50 each."

"Plus utilities," Don added.

"Still manageable. Let's check it out."

The apartment was in a decent complex called Brookhurst Manor. Nothing fancy, but clean and well-maintained. The manager, a middle-aged woman named Mrs. Patterson, showed us around the unit.

"It's been freshly painted," she said, opening the door to reveal beige walls and brown carpeting. "Two bedrooms, one bathroom, kitchen with all appliances included."

The place smelled like fresh paint and carpet cleaner. The living room was small but had a sliding glass door that opened onto a tiny patio. Both bedrooms were about the same size, maybe ten by twelve feet.

"We'll take it," I said, probably too quickly.

Mrs. Patterson smiled. "Excellent. I'll need first month's rent plus a $200 security deposit."

Don and I looked at each other. We'd brought cash, expecting this moment.

"No problem," Don said, pulling out his wallet.

Within an hour, we had keys to our first apartment. I felt like I was holding my freedom in my hand.

Moving day was scheduled for the following Saturday. Don and I rented a U-Haul truck from the place on Foothill Boulevard. When we got to my house that morning, my parents had already left for the gallery. I hadn't planned it that way, but it worked out perfectly.

"Looks like we have the place to ourselves," Don said as we pulled into the empty driveway.

"Good," I said, unlocking the front door. "Less complicated this way."

Loading all my stuff took most of the morning because I'd accumulated a ridiculous amount of junk over the years. Books, records, computer printouts, model kits, clothes, and about fifty pounds of random electronic components I was convinced I'd need someday.

"Jesus, Richard," Don said, lifting a box that rattled with loose parts. "What's in here, an entire radio shop?"

"Resistors, capacitors, some integrated circuits," I said. "You never know when you might need a 555 timer."

"Right," Don said, shaking his head.

I emptied my bedroom completely but left some stuff in the basement. Old textbooks, winter clothes, things I figured I could retrieve later once I was settled.

By noon, the truck was packed solid. We'd managed to Tetris everything into the cargo space, with the heavier furniture on the bottom and boxes stacked to the ceiling. I scribbled a quick note on a piece of paper and left it on the kitchen table:

"Moved out today. Starting my new job Monday. Will call you later. -Richard"

It wasn't that I was trying to sneak out. It just happened that they weren't there, and I didn't see any point in waiting around for a big scene. This was simpler.

Next, we drove to Don's house in San Bernardino to load his stuff. That was relatively easy since Don was a minimalist compared to me. A few boxes of clothes, some books, his stereo system, and a small television. We were done in an hour.

The drive to Orange County felt like the longest trip of my life. Every mile took me further from the cold, silent house where I'd felt like a prisoner. The U-Haul had no air conditioning, and the vinyl seats stuck to our backs in the heat, but I didn't care.

"This thing drives like a tank," Don yelled over the noise of the truck's engine.

"At least it's running," I shouted back.

We arrived at the apartment complex as the sun was setting. Unloading was brutal work, but every piece of furniture we carried up those stairs felt like another step toward independence. By the time we finished, it was past 10:00 PM, and we were both exhausted and covered in sweat.

Just as we were carrying in the last box, we heard sirens. Lots of them. The sound started distant but grew louder until it was deafening.

"What the hell?" Don said, setting down his box.

We looked down the street and saw about a dozen police cars screaming past our complex, red and blue lights flashing. They disappeared around a corner, but the sirens kept wailing.

A few minutes later, we heard gunshots. Pop, pop, pop. Then shouting, curses, and the crackling of police radios echoing off the buildings.

Don and I looked at each other, both thinking the same thing.

"What have we gotten ourselves into?" I said.

"Maybe we should have asked more questions about the neighborhood," Don replied, scanning the street nervously.

We hurried inside with the last of our belongings and locked the door. Through our living room window, we could see more police cars arriving, their headlights sweeping across the apartment buildings.

The next morning, Mrs. Patterson filled us in on the excitement. There had been a shootout at a restaurant about three blocks away. Some guy had tried to rob the place, panicked when the police showed up, and started firing shots in their direction. Nobody was hurt. The criminal had eventually surrendered after running out of ammunition.

"It's not usually this exciting around here," she assured us. "That was the first incident like that in over two years."

But sitting in our new living room, surrounded by boxes and mismatched furniture, I felt something I hadn't felt in years: hope. This was mine. I'd done it. I was out.

I later found out my parents had made a bet that I'd come crawling back to them on my belly, begging, within two weeks. They thought I couldn't survive on my own, that I'd fail and have to return home humiliated.

I'd rather have lived in a trash container.

For the first time in my life, I was truly free.

Epilogue: Building a Life

And with that, I closed the book on that part of my life. Childhood was over. I'm counting childhood from when I was born until I moved out at nineteen. That's when I was able to start becoming a man.

A lot happened after that escape to Orange County. I remained at Software Techniques for about six years, and it became the foundation for everything that followed. After my first year, Rick called me into his office one afternoon.

"Richard, we need to talk," he said, gesturing to the chair across from his desk.

My stomach dropped. In my experience, "we need to talk" usually meant trouble.

"The partners and I have been discussing your performance," Rick continued. "We're promoting you to Vice President of Consulting."

I nearly fell out of my chair. "Vice President? Are you serious?"

"Dead serious. You've earned it. You understand the technology, the clients trust you, and you know how to manage projects. We want you to start building a consulting team."

At twenty years old, I was managing eight people on a huge variety of projects: designing and writing entire accounting systems, apartment management systems, and SCADA systems that controlled everything for several water districts. It was an amazing job working for amazing people.

I need to point out Steve Davis especially. He was the only manager in my entire career who took the time to be a real mentor and teach me what I needed to know to succeed. He was patient, coached me appropriately, chewed me out when necessary, and was an all-around wonderful person to work with.

"Management isn't about being the smartest person in the room," Steve told me during one of our weekly meetings. "It's about helping other people be their best. Your job is to remove obstacles, provide resources, and give people room to succeed."

"What if they make mistakes?" I asked.

"They will make mistakes. You made mistakes. I made mistakes. The question is: are they learning from them?"

Steve later went on to become an executive vice president at Disney and became famous for the work he did there. But I'll always remember him as the guy who taught a scared kid from a dysfunctional family how to be a leader.

After I left Software Techniques, I decided to take two jobs simultaneously. One was working for BIF Actutel, which used to make butterfly valves for nuclear power plants. Since that market dried up after Three Mile Island, they'd pivoted to creating SCADA systems for water management. I was in charge of projects in New Haven, Connecticut; Ojai, California; and Las Vegas Valley Water District.

For several months, I commuted weekly between Las Vegas and Camarillo, where I'd moved. Flying out Sunday night, working in Vegas all week, flying back Friday evening. It sounds glamorous, but living in hotels and eating room service gets old fast.

At the same time, I took a position at Beck Computer Systems as their Vice President of Consulting. It was the same kind of role I'd had at Software Techniques, managing teams of various sizes working on custom software projects.

After about a year and a half of this double life, I did the math and realized something depressing.

"I'm making less money working two jobs than I would working just one," I told Don over lunch one day.

"How is that possible?" he asked.

"Taxes. The IRS treats me like I'm making twice as much money, so I'm in a higher tax bracket. Plus the travel expenses are killing me."

I quit the BIF job and focused on Beck Computer Systems for the next six years.

From there, I made the leap to Trader Joe's. One of our clients, US Growers, recommended me when Trader Joe's was looking for someone to modernize their computer systems. The interview with Fred Morseheimer went well.

"We're not just a grocery store," Fred explained during our meeting. "We're a unique culture. Are you prepared to learn a different way of doing business?"

"I've spent my career adapting to different industries," I said. "Water management, manufacturing, consulting. I learn fast."

"Good. Because you'll be responsible for keeping our entire operation running. Eight warehouses, hundreds of stores, millions of transactions every day."

I spent twenty years at Trader Joe's, almost to the day. Within a few months of starting, I married Claudia, a nice woman I'd met through friends. She had a laugh that could light up a room.

"You know what I love about you?" she told me one evening as we walked on the beach in Santa Monica.

"My devastating good looks?" I said.

"Your intensity. When you care about something, you care completely. Most people go through life half-committed to everything. You don't do anything halfway."

She was right. When I committed to something, whether it was a job, a project, or a relationship, I was all in.

Claudia remained my wife for twelve and a half years until she passed away on January 31, 2005, at 9:57 in the morning at Queen of Angels hospital in Los Angeles. The cause was sepsis, lung disease, and a cascade of other complications. She'd been chronically ill for eight years, and I became her primary caretaker. Watching someone you love slowly deteriorate is its own special kind of hell, but I never considered leaving her side.

"You don't have to do this," she told me during one of her hospitalizations. "I'd understand if..."

"Stop," I said. "We're in this together. That's what 'in sickness and in health' means."

"I know, but I never expected it to be this hard."

"Neither did I. But here we are."

Once she passed, I decided I was not in favor of grief. Instead of wallowing, I started hiking and photographing. I hiked every single National Park and State Park in the Southwest United States, photographing them all. I was drawn to Joshua Tree National Park, where I hiked fifty-two times, taking tens of thousands of photographs.

The desert became my therapy. Something about the vast emptiness and stark beauty helped process emotions I couldn't handle any other way. Every sunrise over the Mojave, every twisted Joshua tree against the sunset, became a meditation on loss and renewal.

I also found myself visiting Renaissance festivals, starting with the Irwindale Renaissance Festival. I'd spend long weekends walking around with my camera, mostly running from grief, photographing everything I could see. I posted all my pictures on a website, creating a record of a world where people celebrated creativity and community.

One day, I was sitting in the back row center seat at a belly dance performance. A woman named Marjhani approached me. She was terrifying to my conservative, sheltered sensibilities: heavily tattooed, pierced, outside my narrow worldview.

She walked up to me, put her arms around me in a hug, and said, "Welcome to the belly dance community. You're welcome at any event, and I'll make sure the front row center seat is always reserved for you."

That simple act of inclusion changed my life. Marjhani and I became best friends, and she introduced me to other dancers who invited me to their shows. This began an eight-year cycle of photographing belly dance events, Renaissance fairs, WWE shows, Ringling Brothers circuses, Mermaid shows, Civil War and World War II reenactments, and other performances.

Each year on my birthday, I threw a huge party and invited all my belly dancer friends. By the time I moved from California, the celebration had expanded to two days with over 200 dancers. I provided the location and catered everything, and they came and performed for me. Many of these people remain dear friends today.

The kid who couldn't make friends, who was too shy to talk to strangers, had somehow built a community of hundreds of creative, passionate people. It took me forty years, but I'd finally learned how to connect with others.

Finally, in 2013, I decided I was tired of working for corporate America. The stress of being on call 24/7, being responsible for multibillion-dollar workflows and computer systems that supported hundreds of stores and eight warehouses, was killing me. The physical and mental damage was becoming undeniable.

So, I quit, moved to Florida, and started my career as a ghostwriter. After some initial struggles with jobs like writing LinkedIn profiles, I found my niche in freelance ghostwriting. I gained several large contracts and built a successful career quickly.

An important fact I didn't realize until recently is that I have ADHD and autism. I don't view that as suffering. They are simply conditions under which I live and that affect my life.

Looking back, I can see how my childhood experiences were a direct cause of the ADHD and autistic conditions. But I can also see the thread that connected it all. That terrified nineteen-year-old who moved out with nothing but a U-Haul full of junk had somehow built a life of independence, achievement, and meaningful relationships. The refuges I'd created as a child, the systems thinking I'd developed to survive chaos, the obsessive attention to detail that had driven my parents crazy, all became the foundation for professional success.

The damage had become the skillset. And somehow, despite everything, it had been enough.

Breaking the Mold: From Victim to Victor

For most of my life, I knew I was different. What I didn't know was why, or that my differences would eventually become my greatest strengths.

Looking back now, I can see the autism, ADHD, and rejection sensitive dysphoria woven throughout my childhood like threads in a tapestry. The hyperfocus that made me spend hours organizing baseball cards wasn't just obsessive behavior. It was my brain's way of creating order in chaos. The social awkwardness that made family gatherings torture wasn't just shyness. It was autism struggling to decode the unwritten rules of a dysfunctional family system. The explosive anger when my father touched me wasn't just teenage rebellion. It was RSD reacting to a lifetime of criticism and rejection.

The collecting wasn't hoarding. It was pattern recognition. My brain was learning to categorize, organize, and find meaning in complexity. Those hours spent arranging rocks, fantasy miniatures, and model kits were training sessions in systematic thinking.

The social struggles weren't character flaws. They were the natural result of an autistic child trying to navigate a family that communicated through emotional warfare and silent treatments. I learned to read the room not through social intuition, but through careful observation and analysis. I developed hypervigilance as a survival skill.

The explosive emotional reactions weren't lack of self-control. They were RSD protecting me from a family that seemed determined to prove I was worthless. Every criticism hit like a physical blow because my brain was wired to interpret rejection as life-threatening. But that same sensitivity also made me fiercely determined to prove them wrong.

The refuge I found in books and fantasy wasn't escapism. It was my brain seeking environments where rules made sense, where logic prevailed, where intelligent, awkward heroes could save the day. I was learning that different worlds were possible.

But here's the crucial part: at some point, I stopped being a victim of my neurodivergence and became its director.

I don't know exactly when the shift happened. Maybe it was when I discovered programming and realized my obsessive attention to detail was a superpower. Maybe it was when I stood up to my father and refused to be his victim anymore. Maybe it was when I walked into that job interview and realized my "weird" skills were exactly what they needed.

But most people don't understand ADHD hyperfocus: it's not just an uncontrollable obsession that happens to you. Once you recognize it for what it is, you can learn to aim it like a firehose. When I need to master a new technology, solve a complex problem, or complete a challenging project, I don't fight my brain's tendency to become absorbed. I direct it.

I've learned to set up the conditions that trigger hyperfocus deliberately. Clear the schedule. Eliminate distractions. Choose the right environment. Then I point that laser-beam intensity exactly where I want it to go. While neurotypical people struggle to maintain focus for hours on complex tasks, I can disappear into a problem for an entire day and emerge with solutions that take others weeks to develop. What looks like a disability to the outside world is a superpower once you learn to control the targeting system. The same brain that made me a "difficult child" allows me to accomplish in days what takes most people months.

I didn't overcome my autism, ADHD, and RSD. I weaponized them.

Every coping mechanism I'd developed became a professional skill. Hyperfocus became deep expertise. Pattern recognition became system design. Hypervigilance became project management. Systematic organization became database architecture. Emotional intensity became leadership presence.

What they saw as damage, I transformed into tools.

This is what it means to be causative instead of reactive. Reactive people say, "This is happening to me, and I can't control it." Causative people say, "This is my raw material, and I decide what to build with it."

They tried to teach me that I was too much: too intense, too obsessive, too sensitive, too different. Instead, I learned that I was exactly enough. Enough to build a career, enough to earn respect, enough to create meaningful relationships, enough to live life on my own terms.

The mold they tried to force me into was too small anyway. Breaking it wasn't failure. It was liberation.

Acknowledgements

Belinda Lowe-Schmahl and Ken Schmahl

My sister Belinda and her husband Ken have built something extraordinary with Schmahl Science Workshops in San Jose. What started in 1994 when Belinda's fourth-grade daughter needed help with a science fair project has grown into one of the most impactful educational nonprofits in Silicon Valley. Belinda, a trained biochemist who had done research at UC Riverside and Cal Poly Pomona, began by inviting her daughter and a few friends into their garage for hands-on science experiments. That simple act of making science fun and accessible has reached over 325,000 children across three decades.

Schmahl Science Workshops now serves 14,000 students annually at 85 schools in 18 districts, focusing on underserved communities in East San Jose and other disadvantaged areas. Their team of 15 instructors includes former scientists from Stanford, NASA, UCLA, UC Berkeley, Oracle, Hewlett Packard, and Apple who bring real-world expertise into elementary classrooms. They've created mobile labs, mentorship programs, and research opportunities that give kids from all backgrounds access to the same quality science education that wealthy districts take for granted. Belinda's philosophy is simple but powerful: "The kids in East Side and downtown San Jose are just as smart as kids in Cupertino." She's spent thirty years proving that point.

What I admire most about Belinda and Ken is that they've taken the same approach to education that I learned to take with my own challenges: they refuse to accept limitations imposed by circumstances. Where others saw disadvantaged kids who couldn't access quality science education, they saw brilliant minds that just needed the right opportunities and resources. They've turned what could have been a barrier into a mission, creating pathways for students who might never have discovered their potential otherwise. Their work embodies the same principle that guided my own transformation: apparent deficits can become superpowers when you refuse to accept that they define your limits. Belinda and Ken have spent three decades proving that every child deserves the chance to fall in love with learning, regardless of where they come from.

Steve Davis

Steve Davis was the only manager in my entire career who took the time to be a real mentor and teach me what I needed to know to succeed. At Software Techniques, he was patient, coached me appropriately, chewed me out when necessary, and was an all-around wonderful person to work with. He taught me that management isn't about being the smartest person in the room, but about helping other people be their best — removing obstacles, providing resources, and giving people room to succeed.

Steve went on to become Chief Architect and Vice President of IT at Walt Disney Studios, where he served on Disney's IT Leadership Board and chaired their Enterprise Architecture Board. He became one of the most respected technology strategists in the industry, developing breakthrough systems: Disney's film distribution system, enterprise architecture frameworks, and the sophisticated guest tracking and analytics systems that revolutionized how Disney understands and serves its customers. In 2010, he was honored with the Computerworld Premier 100 IT Leadership Award for transforming how one of the world's largest entertainment companies used technology.

The same patient mentorship he showed me at Software Techniques, he applied to building world-class technology teams at Disney. He holds multiple patents and developed some of the first disk defragmentation software, operating system extensions, and user-based licensing models that became industry standards. Looking back, I wasn't just learning management skills from Steve. I was learning from someone who would go on to architect the technological backbone of the most successful entertainment company in the world. I'll always remember him as the guy who taught a scared kid from a dysfunctional family how to be a leader.

John Shields

John Shields became my boss at Trader Joe's when my previous manager left, and he taught me the difference between management and true leadership. John spent his time in the stores asking employees a simple but powerful question: "What are we doing at the office to screw you up?" He filled twenty notepads with the answers, then systematically removed those obstacles. John didn't act like a typical manager because he understood that his job wasn't to control people, but to create an environment where they could succeed. He was famous for saying he wouldn't hire anyone in retail who didn't smile within thirty seconds of meeting them, not because he wanted fake cheerfulness, but because he believed that genuine enthusiasm was essential for creating the Trader Joe's culture.

John had an extraordinary career in retail, starting at Macy's in 1958 and rising to Senior Vice President of Operations after twenty years. He then moved to Mervyn's, where he held similar leadership roles until retiring in 1987. His retirement lasted exactly five weeks before his old Stanford fraternity brother Joe Coulombe asked him to consult for Trader Joe's. That consulting assignment led to John becoming CEO when Coulombe retired, and under his leadership from 1988 to 2001, Trader Joe's exploded from 27 West Coast stores to a national chain of 174 stores in thirteen states. Sales grew from $132 million to over $2 billion during his tenure.

What made John exceptional wasn't just his business success, but his philosophy that work should be enjoyable and meaningful for everyone involved. He was named Master Entrepreneur of the Los Angeles Area in 1993 and Retailer of the Year by the Institute of Retail Management, but he never let success change his fundamental approach to leadership. John understood that creating a great company meant creating a great culture first, then trusting that culture to drive business results. He taught me that true leadership isn't about having all the answers, but about asking the right questions and then listening carefully to what your people tell you. The lessons I learned from John about servant leadership influenced every management decision I made for the rest of my career.

Jannah

I want to acknowledge Jannah, who taught me that genuine friendship between men and women is not only possible but can be one of the most rewarding relationships you can have. I met her at a belly dance show in 2006, during one of the darkest periods of my life after Claudia's death. Where most people might have offered sympathy or tried to fix my grief, Jannah did something better: she balanced her sword on her head, did some belly dance moves, and loudly interrupted the show we were watching. We were so rowdy we almost got kicked out, but she cheered me up in a way that felt genuine and unforced.

What made our friendship extraordinary was that we had the conversation most men and women never have: we talked honestly about what we wanted from each other. Jannah made it clear she wasn't interested in anything romantic, and I wasn't ready for anything serious either. So we agreed to be friends. Real friends. Not the kind where I was secretly hoping for more, or where she was using me for emotional support while dating other guys. We were both honest about our intentions, respected each other's boundaries, and treated each other as equals. This friendship lasted over a decade, through annual cruises, trips to the Grand Canyon, and countless shows and festivals.

Jannah showed me that women are interesting people when you start appreciating them as people. She had insights, opinions, and experiences that enriched my life in ways that had nothing to do with romance. She was direct, honest, and didn't expect me to read her mind or solve her problems. Our friendship proved that the most satisfying relationships aren't always romantic ones, and that the key to understanding women better is learning how to be genuine friends with them first. Most men miss out on this because they can't get past their own agenda, but Jannah taught me that their loss is profound. She remains one of the most important people in my life, not despite the fact that our relationship was purely platonic, but because of it.

Marjhani

I need to acknowledge Marjhani BellaMorte, the woman who changed my life by doing something incredibly simple: she welcomed me. When I showed up at the Irwindale Renaissance Festival in 2005, still raw from grief and completely out of my element, I was this conservative, sheltered guy who had no business being around heavily tattooed, pierced belly dancers.

Marjhani was terrifying to my narrow worldview, but she walked up to me, put her arms around me, and said, "Welcome to the belly dance community. You're welcome at any event, and I'll make sure the front row center seat is always reserved for you." That simple act of inclusion opened a door I didn't even know existed.

With over 20 years of belly dance experience and 35 years on goth club dance floors, this world-renowned performer who had taught and danced around the world and led the belly dance group at the Original Renaissance Faire from 2005-2008, took one look at this awkward outsider with a camera and decided I belonged. Marjhani introduced me to other dancers, helped me understand the community, and became the bridge between my isolated existence and a world full of creative, passionate people. She taught me that sometimes the most important thing you can do for someone is simply tell them they're welcome exactly as they are.

Mardhavi Sakuntala

I want to acknowledge Mardhavi, a multi-talented artist who embodies everything I love about the creative community I found after Claudia's death. As a percussionist, film composer, songwriter, producer, DJ, Bharata Natyam dancer, bellydancer, and yogini, she represents the kind of passionate, multi-faceted creativity that drew me into the Renaissance and belly dance world.

Her South Asian/Middle Eastern musical fusion as Saltation Ignite, her commitment to feminism, animal rights, environmental protection, and social justice, and her identity as a spontaneous, artsy, free-spirited "somewhat weird grrrl" made her exactly the kind of person I needed to meet during my journey from isolation to community. But Mardhavi became more than just another creative friend. When I decided to leave California and move to Florida in 2013, she accompanied me on that long cross-country drive, helping me navigate both the physical journey and the emotional transition of leaving my old life behind.

Later that year, she came back out to Florida in November, fresh from a gig in Jamaica, just to cook me a vegan Thanksgiving turkey. That gesture captured who she is: someone who travels the world pursuing her art but still makes time to care for the people in her life. Mardhavi proved that the creative community I'd found wasn't just about shared interests, but about genuine friendship and support when it mattered most.

Dr. Young - History Professor

Dr. Young was the rare college professor who cared more about teaching students to think than forcing them to memorize facts. In his Western Civilization class, he challenged us to see the Bible as a historical document shaped by political forces rather than divine revelation, sparking heated debates that taught me more about critical thinking than any other course I took. While other professors obsessed over dates and names, Dr. Young focused on understanding why things happened and how ideas evolved over centuries. His willingness to tackle controversial subjects and encourage dissent showed me that education could be about questioning accepted narratives rather than just absorbing them. He proved that the best teachers don't give you answers - they teach you how to ask better questions.

Bob - College Friend and Collecting Mentor

Bob introduced me to the world of systematic collecting and showed me that friendship could be based on shared obsessions rather than social skills. Through role-playing games and detailed discussions about fantasy worlds, he taught me that it was possible to connect with someone who understood my need to organize, categorize, and master complex systems. Bob represented something rare in my experience: a friend who appreciated my intensity and analytical thinking instead of seeing them as character flaws.

While I was socially awkward and struggled with typical teenage interactions, Bob proved that finding your tribe meant finding people who shared your interests and accepted your differences. He helped me understand that being weird wasn't a problem if you could find other people who were weird in compatible ways.

Don - The Friend Who Changed Everything

Don was the college friend who made the phone call that changed the trajectory of my life. When Rick needed to hire someone at Software Techniques, Don recommended me without hesitation, giving me the opportunity to escape my toxic home situation and start building a career. That simple act of friendship - seeing potential in someone and being willing to vouch for them - demonstrated how one person's belief in you can open doors you didn't even know existed. Don proved that sometimes the most important thing a friend can do is connect you with opportunities that match your abilities, even when you can't see those abilities clearly yourself.

David - Childhood Best Friend

David was my window into what normal family life could look like, showing me that homes could be places where valuable things were protected and displayed rather than broken during arguments. His Jewish family's careful preservation of religious artifacts in glass cases taught me that collections could be statements about what you valued, not just accumulated clutter. David accepted my intensity and interests without trying to change me, proving that friendship didn't require fitting into predetermined social molds. Through our relationship, I learned that some families actually respected their children's differences and encouraged their interests instead of seeing them as problems to be solved.

Grandfather - The Unbroken Survivor

My maternal grandfather was the only family member I truly respected, a man who survived four years as a Japanese prisoner of war and emerged with his integrity intact. His quiet dignity in the face of grandmother's constant belittling showed me what real strength looked like - not the explosive violence of my father, but the steady resilience of someone who refused to let trauma turn him bitter. Grandfather taught me that survival wasn't just about enduring hardship, but about maintaining your principles under pressure. His stories of organizing fair food distribution and protecting weaker prisoners during his captivity revealed a man who understood that true leadership means taking care of others, even when you're struggling yourself.

You can read about Grandfathers POW story in my book "Behind the Wire", available on Amazon.

Uncle Frank - The Family Truth-Teller

Frank was the one family member who had successfully escaped the dysfunction and could articulate exactly what was wrong with our family system. While everyone else warned me to stay away from him, calling him "weird," Frank's weirdness was actually his refusal to participate in the family's victim narratives and manipulation games. He offered practical help and honest guidance when I was confused by the toxic dynamics around me, serving as proof that it was possible to break free from generational patterns of dysfunction. Frank's independence and clear-eyed assessment of family problems gave me hope that escape was possible and showed me what life could look like when you refused to accept limitations imposed by others.

Claudia

I want to acknowledge Claudia, my wife of twelve and a half years, who taught me what commitment means even when circumstances become difficult. She had a brilliant mind that could solve problems I couldn't even understand and a laugh that could light up a room.

During our early years together, she helped me recognize my own intensity as a strength instead of a flaw, telling me, "When you care about something, you care completely. Most people go through life half-committed to everything. You don't do anything halfway." That insight became central to how I understood myself and approached everything that followed.

When she became chronically ill for the final eight years of our marriage, I learned what "in sickness and in health" truly meant. Caring for someone through a long, difficult illness tests every assumption you have about love, patience, and endurance. Those years taught me that sometimes the most important thing you can do for another person is simply refuse to give up on them, even when they offer you an easy way out.

After her death, I discovered that grief could be transformed into something creative and connecting instead of just endured, leading me to photography and the artistic community that became central to my later life. Claudia's death marked the end of one chapter but became the catalyst for discovering capacities I didn't know I had.

About the Author

Richard Lowe spent the first nineteen years of his life surviving what he calls "Crazytown," a dysfunctional family system that would have broken most people. Instead, it forged him into one of the most successful ghostwriters and systems thinkers of his generation.

Born at Travis Air Force Base to parents whose toxic relationship would define his childhood, Richard learned early that survival required developing mental refuges and systematic thinking. What others saw as problems (his intense focus, pattern recognition abilities, and emotional distance) became the foundation for an extraordinary career.

After escaping his family situation at nineteen with nothing but a U-Haul full of belongings, Richard built a remarkable professional life. He started at Software Techniques, where he was promoted to Vice President of Consulting at just twenty years old, managing complex projects for water districts, government agencies, and private corporations. His systematic approach to problem-solving and ability to design elegant software solutions established his reputation in the technology sector.

Richard spent six years at Software Techniques before taking simultaneous positions at BIF Actutel (working on SCADA systems for water management) and Beck Computer Systems. His career culminated in a twenty-year tenure at Trader Joe's, where he was responsible for the computer systems supporting eight warehouses, hundreds of stores, and millions of daily transactions.

Throughout his corporate career, Richard demonstrated an unusual ability to translate complex technical concepts into practical business solutions. His mentors, including Steve Davis (who later became an executive vice president at Disney), recognized that Richard's apparent differences were sophisticated capabilities that made him valuable in high-stakes environments.

After his wife Claudia died on January 31, 2005, at Queen of Angels hospital in Los Angeles, Richard discovered photography and community building, creating networks of creative professionals and documenting Renaissance festivals, belly dance performances, and other cultural events across the country. His annual birthday celebrations grew from small gatherings to two-day events featuring over 200 performers.

In 2013, Richard retired from corporate life and moved to Florida to pursue full-time ghostwriting. His combination of technical expertise, systematic thinking, and deep understanding of human psychology made him skilled at helping clients organize their thoughts and find their authentic voices. He built a successful freelance practice, working with entrepreneurs, executives, and thought leaders to transform their ideas into compelling written works.

Richard's recent recognition that he has ADHD and autism reframed his entire life story. He doesn't see these as disabilities to overcome, but as the source of his greatest professional strengths. His hypervigilance became project management skills. His pattern recognition became systems design expertise. His emotional intensity became leadership presence.

Welcome to Crazytown represents Richard's belief that what we call "damage" can become our most valuable skillset when placed in the right context. He currently lives in Florida, where he continues his ghostwriting practice and advocates for understanding neurodivergence as a source of capability.

Richard's story proves that the traits that make you an outsider in one environment can make you essential in another, and that the worst things that happen to you can become the best things about you.

Books by Richard Lowe

See books by Richard Lowe at

https://masterofworlds.com

Get free publishing insights and industry updates at

https://thewritingking.substack.com

For ghostwriting and book coaching services see

https://thewritingking.com

www.ingramcontent.com/pod-product-compliance
Lightning Source LLC
Chambersburg PA
CBHW020911060726
47591CB00004B/1193